The beginner's guide to MICROWAVE COOKERY

Val Collins

D1340102

DAVID & CHARLES
Newton Abbot   London   North Pomfret (Vt)

Selection of fresh fruit, vegetables, meat and fish

First published 1982
Second impression 1984
Printed in The Netherlands
by Smeets Offset BV, Weert
for David & Charles (Publishers) Limited
Brunel House Newton Abbot Devon

Published in the United States of America
by David & Charles Inc
North Pomfret Vermont 05053 USA

British Library Cataloguing in Publication Data

Collins, Val
    The beginner's guide to microwave cookery.
    1. Microwave cookery
    I. Title
    641.5′882   TX832
ISBN 0–7153–8316–7

To my niece Eleanor

Contents

Introduction

I have been using microwave cookers now for so many years that I think I take all the advantages they offer me for granted. Rather like the freezer, a microwave cooker is now so much a part of my kitchen and daily life that it is difficult for me to remember how I ever coped without it.

On thinking back to the early days when first introduced to the idea of 'cooking by microwave', I too had all the doubts and questions that I'm sure you have considered – 'Is it safe? Will it cook a jacket potato, or a cake, defrost and cook a chicken, reheat a sausage roll?' The answer to all these is 'yes'. And because a microwave cooker is so adaptable, it will cook many other dishes that you may not even have thought of, from something as simple as scrambled eggs in two to three minutes, to a Christmas pudding in six.

Prime cooking operations – thawing, melting, poaching, boiling, simmering, roasting and baking – can be carried out in seconds and minutes rather than minutes and hours, with no more effort than it takes to place the food in the oven and operate the controls. Because food is cooked so quickly, fewer valuable nutrients are lost and as all the heat is produced in the food itself and is not wasted elsewhere, this means that the microwave cooker is also very economical to use. On average, up to 75 per cent can be saved on normal cooking times and up to 50 per cent of your cooking fuel bill. Food can be cooked and served in one dish, so saving on the washing up; also, as little heat is produced in the oven, the kitchen will remain cooler and cleaner too.

In a nutshell, a microwave cooker gives you a more nutritious meal, cooked more quickly thus using less electricity, and after the meal there are fewer dishes to wash up and a cool oven which cleans with a wipe.

The microwave cooker is easy to install – you just plug it into a 13 amp or 15 amp socket outlet which means that it can be situated in the kitchen, in the dining room, or on a trolley so it may be wheeled from room to room, or even out on to the patio to assist with the barbecue. With no temperatures to set, only timer controls to adjust, the microwave cooker is so simple to operate that any member of the family can reheat cooked meals or snacks left for them, in the refrigerator or freezer, when they arrive home late.

As you use the microwave cooker more and more you will find that you use your conventional cooker less often, although you will still need it for some foods that the microwave cooker just cannot cope with – Yorkshire puddings, pancakes, roast potatoes, some pastries and foods that are deep fat fried, for example. But as a complement to the conventional cooker, refrigerator and freezer, a microwave cooker will make life easier for all those of you involved in the preparation and cooking of food.

I have written this book as a guide for those of you taking your first steps in microwave cookery. You will find the section 'Simple Beginnings' particularly useful and helpful in getting to know your microwave cooker. Whichever model you have chosen, this book gives all the basic information and will enable you and your family to benefit and enjoy all your favourite dishes – as well as some new ones – cooked in a fraction of the time normally spent in meal preparation.

The microwave cooker

The original microwave cookers were developed as a result of research into radar during the second world war, the first model being produced in America in the late 1940s. Since the launch of the first domestic model in the mid 1950s, it has become accepted as a new concept in cooking and is definitely here to stay as an adjunct to other kitchen appliances.

New and recent developments have made a wide choice of models available. Standard units with on/off controls have been introduced with additional features such as defrost controls, selector or variable power controls, turntables, browning elements and temperature probes. The control panel on a microwave cooker consists mainly of one or two timers, a defrost control and/or variable power control, indicator lights and a start or cook button. There are some models with sophisticated electronic programming and sensing devices, and touch control systems. With no knobs, dials or switches, the cooker is operated by simply touching the appropriate section of the control panel.

The timer control is most important – microwave cooking is gauged by time, not time and temperature

– and is marked so that the shorter heating or cooking periods can be set with a degree of accuracy. The variable power and defrost controls are explained more fully in their relevant sections (pages 14 and 15 respectively) but basically they allow a greater flexibility of the cooking speed by varying the energy or power level flowing into the oven cavity, which may be compared with the equivalent of conventional oven settings. With many food items this is unnecessary but it can be invaluable for those foods or dishes which may benefit from a longer, slower cooking period.

In some models, cooking commences when the start or cook button is operated; in others, when the timer is set. On completion of cooking, an audible warning indicates that the set cooking period has elapsed and the cooker turns itself off. Alternatively, the cooker may be switched off at any time during a cooking operation by turning the timer back to zero or by simply opening the oven door. Incorporated into the door mechanism are safety interlock microswitches which break contact when the door is opened; any one of the microswitches will ensure that the microwave energy is switched off and that the oven is no longer operating. Conversely, if one of the microswitches does not make contact when the door is closed, then the microwave cooker cannot be operated.

Before you first use your microwave cooker it is important to know how it operates and to understand all the facts given in the manufacturer's instructions. These give detailed information on the installation, operation and care of your particular model and should be read through carefully. Although you may accept delivery of a new appliance into your kitchen without too much concern for the technological background, knowing that years of research and experience have ensured that it will be functional and give satisfactory service, a microwave cooker by these standards is still relatively new so I thought it might be of interest to you to know something of its behaviour, and about microwave energy – what it is and how it works.

Microwave energy

The method of applying energy in the form of heat to cook food has hardly changed at all since early man first accidentally dropped a piece of meat into the open fire and found out that it tasted better cooked than raw. To cook food placed in a conventional oven, whether it be electric, gas or solid fuel, depends on conduction from the source of the heat to the surface and then the inside of the food. To accelerate cooking, the source of the heat or oven temperature may be increased but this can cause excessive browning or overcooking of the outside of the food. Unlike conventional ovens, microwave cookers heat and cook food without applying external heat, but by applying microwave energy.

What is microwave energy?
Microwaves – or microwave energy – are electromagnetic, non-ionising high-frequency radio waves, close to but not as powerful as infra-red rays. They must NOT be confused with X rays, gamma rays, or ultra-violet rays, which are ionising and are known to cause irreversible chemical and cellular changes to take place with little or no temperature change. Of equal importance, microwaves are non-cumulative.

The worst thing that could happen if one was accidentally exposed to microwave energy would be a nasty burn and you would feel it just as if you had placed a hand or finger into a naked flame. It is far more dangerous to sunbathe in the direct glare of the sun for hours on end or subject oneself to a sunlamp. Protection from unnecessary exposure to microwave energy is a requirement in all microwave cookers.

Statutory electrical safety standards and modern technology have ensured that cut-out microswitches are built in and operate as soon as the door is opened, so that the microwave energy switches off immediately. It will not start again until the door is securely shut and the start button operated. The microwave cooker door is built to precise specifications to ensure that, when shut, the oven cavity is effectively sealed against energy leakage. Cooking by microwave is safe – frequently safer than cooking conventionally when you take into consideration the relative lack of heat and, therefore, practically no risk of conventional accidental skin burns.

How it works
In the diagram the main components of the microwave cooker are identified, although some may vary between different manufacturers' designs and models.
When the plug top (1) is inserted into the socket outlet

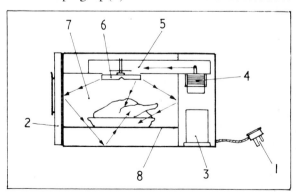

and is switched on, it enables the microwave cooker to be operated. As soon as the controls have been set and the oven door (2) is closed, the cooker may be switched on and the energy begin to flow. The main function of the transformer (3) is to convert the low voltage of the domestic electrical supply to the high voltages required by the microwave-energy generator or magnetron (4).

When microwaves are produced by the magnetron, this energy is directed along the waveguide (5) into the oven cavity via the stirrer blade (6) which ensures an even distribution of the microwaves throughout the oven cavity (7). The microwave energy is then absorbed by the food placed on the oven shelf (8). Some models do not incorporate a stirrer blade but depend on a revolving turntable at shelf level to turn the food through the microwave energy. Other models include a stirrer blade *and* a turntable, which reduces the necessity of turning a dish during a heating or cooking process (page 13).

Microwaves are reflected from some materials such as metal and foil and, therefore, are also reflected from the metal construction of the oven cavity, but will pass through such materials as glass, china, pottery, paper and some plastics, all of which make excellent cooking utensils for use in the microwave oven.

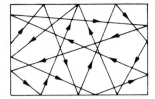 

Materials with a high water content, like most foods, absorb microwave energy and the effect of this absorption on those foods is a rise in temperature. Microwaves vibrate millions of times per second; that is, they have a high frequency and very short wave length (hence the term microwave). As the electromagnetic waves at a frequency of 2,450 mega Hz enter the food, the molecules tend to align themselves with the energy and thus move rapidly back and forth. This high speed causes friction between the molecules, converting the microwave energy into heat to cook food quickly and efficiently.

A similar effect can be made by rubbing your hands together – see how warm they become. We physically experience a similar phenomenon when we stand before a window on a cold, sunny day. The sun generates energy in the form of heat which is radiated through space to the surface of the earth. These rays pass through the glass window without heating it and it feels cold to the touch but the molecules in our body behave like tiny magnets and convert the sun's energy into heat and our body feels warm.

A characteristic of microwave energy is its ability to penetrate food materials to a depth of approximately 2.5 centimetres (1 inch) and produce heat instantaneously; consequently the outer surface of the food may receive more heat than the centre. This is why some recipes will recommend the stirring or turning of foods during cooking and a heat 'equalising' or 'standing' time is suggested on the completion of some microwave cooking to allow heat to be conducted from the outside of the food through to the centre.

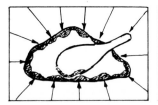 

Never operate the microwave cooker when the oven is empty. If there is nothing to absorb the microwave energy, then the microwaves will bounce off the cavity walls and reflect back onto the magnetron, thereby shortening its life. A wise precaution would be to leave a cup of water in the oven when it is not in use, just in case the cooker is switched on accidentally.

Utensils

One of the advantages of microwave cooking is that foods may be cooked and served in the same dish. Also, owing to the fact that heat is produced within the food itself, nothing burns on, so containers are generally easier to clean and food tends not to stick.

Microwave energy is reflected from metal, which means that aluminium, aluminium foil, tin, copper and stainless steel containers must *not* be used. However, microwave energy passes through glass, pottery and china and so, provided they have no metal trim, they all make excellent containers when cooking in the microwave oven.

Some pottery and china absorb more microwave energy which makes them less efficient. If in doubt, it is worth checking a container by carrying out a simple test. Place the dish in question into the microwave together with a glass of water. After 1½ minutes cooking time the water should be hot and the dish cool. If the reverse is found then the dish must not be used. On the other hand, if the dish and the water are both warm, then the dish could be used, but as it is absorbing some microwave energy it is less efficient and cooking times would be longer. Most dishes remain cool as microwave energy passes through them to be absorbed by the food, but during cooking

Fondue (page 33) and Mulled Wine (page 25)

there may be some heat transfer from the food to the dish so be careful when handling them.

To the new microwave user, I normally recommend sorting through the containers and dishes you already have, before embarking on the puchase of new ones. Quite often it is possible to improvise – most cupboards have an assortment of glass or pottery bowls and pie dishes for fruit puddings and crumbles. Ovenproof glass and pottery flan dishes can be used equally well in the conventional oven or the microwave cooker for tarts or quiches; also oven-to-table casserole dishes are excellent for microwave cooking. Roasting bags and boiling bags are ideal for cooking some foods as they can be easily shaken or turned over to stir the contents during the cooking process. Remember, however, that the wire ties supplied with some makes must not be used. Rubber bands or string ties make suitable alternatives and the bag should be tied loosely to allow some steam to escape. The food will remain hot for a considerable time after cooking if the bag is not opened. It is, therefore, possible to cook several items of food one after another and serve them together.

Shapes and sizes
Generally, the more regular the shape of the container the better it is for even heating or cooking. A round dish is preferable to an oval one and a straight-sided dish better than one which is curved. A container which is slightly rounded at the corners rather than one with square corners will help to prevent food from overcooking at these sharper edges. Larger, shallow dishes are preferable to smaller, deep ones as the greater surface area allows more penetration of the microwave energy. It is important to ensure that the container is large enough to hold the food to be heated or cooked. Pudding mixtures in particular rise extremely well – to almost double their volume – so remember to only half fill the container with the uncooked mixture.

7

Special microwave containers

There is now a wide choice of special microwave cooking containers and dishes available on the market, but a selection would depend on your needs and requirements. Some of these utensils are intended for conventional as well as microwave cooking, while others are suitable for both microwave and the freezer, which are added advantages.

Browning dishes see page 10.

Glass

Any type of glass utensil may be used providing there is no metal trim. Thus glass ovenware – eg Pyrex dishes, jugs, casseroles, plates, tumblers and bowls – can be used. Ceramic glass dishes such as Pyroflam also function extremely well in microwave cooking and make attractive serving dishes.

China and pottery

These can be used in the same way as oven glassware providing there is no metal trim or manufacturer's mark or design in gold or silver. This can cause arcing – blue flashes of light – when the metal trim or pattern will discolour and peel. Some pottery can absorb more microwave energy than others, which slows down the cooking thus making these containers less efficient. They also may become fairly hot to the touch and the use of oven gloves is advisable.

Plastic

Rigid plastic or heat resistant plastic dinnerware can be used but may absorb some microwave energy and will be hotter to the touch than other dishes. Freezer containers or lightweight plastic containers can be used for short periods but the heat from the food they contain can cause them to melt during prolonged exposure to microwaves.

Do not use cream cartons, yoghurt pots or plastic bags as they will melt, but the 'boil-in' type bags are excellent although you must remember to prick them to allow steam to escape.

Do not use plastic or plastic freezer bags in the microwave cooker although frozen food wrapped in plastic bags may be placed into the oven for a short period in order to loosen the package before transferring its contents to another more suitable container.

Paper

Many individual servings of food may be heated on serviettes or paper plates. Frozen gateaux, pastries, sandwiches etc may be placed on paper doyleys before defrosting in the microwave oven. Kitchen paper towels can be used to absorb moisture. Greasproof paper can be used to cover food to prevent splashing in the oven, but kitchen paper towels are just as good and normally less expensive. Do not however place coloured or patterned kitchen paper towels close to food items as the colour may transfer on to the food.

Wax-coated paper cups, plates and paper may be used for short periods only, as prolonged heating may cause the wax to melt.

Do not use paper and metal twist ties as they can burn very quickly. Make sure they are removed from plastic freezer bags before placing in the microwave oven to loosen.

Wicker and straw baskets

These may be used in the microwave for short-term heating only as long exposure to microwave energy may cause them to dry out and crack. However, they are absolutely ideal when thawing or reheating bread or rolls before a meal or dinner party.

Heatproof spatulas and wooden spoons

Plastic spatulas and wooden spoons may be used in the microwave cooker for stirring and mixing. If wooden spoons have absorbed grease or moisture they will become hot.

Clingfilm

This is excellent for covering dishes and plate meals; however, as it is inclined to stretch and dilate during cooking due to the steam trapped underneath, it is advisable to slit the clingfilm with a knife or scissors before placing the dish in the microwave cooker. This is not necessary though when proving dough in the microwave cooker.

Linings

The use of clingfilm to line dishes has the advantage of enabling delicate cakes and puddings to be removed more easily from the container (especially when still warm) and placed the right way up on the cooling rack. Also it practically eliminates the need to wash the dish afterwards. The one disadvantage of using clingfilm as a lining is that it is sometimes difficult to obtain neat corners and edges which may be important to the shape of the cooked result. In this case, it is preferable to line the base of the greased dish with greaseproof paper. It is better not to dust with flour, as this is inclined to result in a doughy crust forming on the outside of the baked product.

Roasting bags and boiling bags

These are extremely convenient for cooking a variety of foods ensuring excellent results. Roasting bags are inclined to enhance the browning of joints and poultry and enable vegetables and fruits to be cooked with very little additional liquid.

Do not use the metal ties provided with the bags; elastic bands or string ties can be used instead.

Metal
Metal pots and pans and other utensils with a high proportion of metal must *not* be used in the microwave oven. This includes tin, aluminium, copper and stainless steel cooking utensils. The reason for their non-use is that microwave energy is reflected from metal, thus preventing the food within the metal container from cooking while the reflected microwave energy may cause damage to the magnetron.

Commercially frozen food in aluminium foil containers should be removed and placed in another dish. Never put an unopened can into the oven – always remove the contents and place in a suitable container.

Aluminium foil
Small smooth pieces may be used to cover bones or narrower ends of poultry, meat or fish for part of the heating or cooking time to prevent overcooking. Care should be taken to ensure the foil is smoothed tightly around the ends. By using aluminium foil in this way you are in fact preventing the microwaves from reaching that area of the food as they are reflected from metal, thus slowing down the cooking time. Foil should not be allowed to touch the sides, rear, top or door of the cooker.

Metal skewers
These may be used if they are placed carefully in large joints. The skewers must not touch one another or the metal sides, rear, top or door of the cooker. Providing these rules are followed, kebab skewers may be used in the microwave oven but if sparking or arcing occurs, rearrange or remove the skewers.

Thermometers
Thermometers which are specially designed for use in the microwave cooker are now available and should be used according to the manufacturer's instructions. Unless specially designed, other meat or sugar thermometers must not be used. Foods can of course be removed from the cooker and checked with a conventional cooking thermometer.

Browning dishes

colour photograph opposite

With a microwave browning dish, it is possible to prepare an entirely new range of dishes in the microwave cooker as it enables some cooked foods to attain the traditional golden-brown appearance normally associated with conventionally cooked foods. The browning dish functions in a similar way to a frying pan or grill and is capable of browning, grilling or searing food items such as beefburgers, steaks, chops and chicken joints; larger joints of meat and poultry brown anyway during their longer cooking time.

Whether the browning dish is used as a skillet or grill, it functions in the same way. In appearance it is a normal glass ceramic or Pyroflam dish but has a tin oxide coating on the base. Unlike the remaining surface of the glass ceramic dish which allows microwaves to pass through, the special coating on the underside of the browning dish absorbs microwaves when preheated. This makes the bottom surface of the preheated empty browning dish very hot. When foods are placed on to the hot surface they brown in the same way as other foods do when added to a hot frying pan.

The temperature of the food, however, cools the browning dish, so the dish will therefore need reheating (for about half the original preheat time) before placing the next batch of food in. Food initially placed on the hot surface browns most attractively. When the dish, containing the food, is placed back in the oven, microwave energy cooks the food while the base of the dish continues to brown the underside.

Preheating

Preheat times vary with the size and shape of the browning dish, the output of the microwave cooker, the type and quantity of the food being cooked and the degree of browning required. Larger browning surfaces require up to 2 minutes longer preheat time than the smaller ones.

It is important to experiment a little when first

Browning dish chart

POWER LEVEL 100% (FULL)

Food	Preheat	Butter or Oil	First Side	Second Side
1 Steak, 175g (6oz)	6–7 min	15g ($\frac{1}{2}$oz) butter or 1 × 15ml tbsp (1 tbsp) oil	$1\frac{1}{2}$–2 min	$1\frac{1}{2}$–2 min
2 Pork chops, each 225g (8oz)	5–6 min	15g ($\frac{1}{2}$oz) butter or 1 × 15ml tbsp (1 tbsp) oil	3 min	8–10 min
4 Beefburgers from frozen	6–7 min	15g ($\frac{1}{2}$oz) butter or 1 × 15ml tbsp (1 tbsp) oil	$1\frac{1}{2}$–2 min	2–3 min
4 Bacon rashers	5–6 min	15g ($\frac{1}{2}$oz) butter or 1 × 15ml tbsp (1 tbsp) oil if required	1 min	30–45 sec
2 Chicken pieces 225g (8oz) each	5–6 min	15g ($\frac{1}{2}$oz) butter or 1 × 15ml tbsp (1 tbsp) oil	5 min	3–5 min
4 Sausages, large	5–6 min	15g ($\frac{1}{2}$oz) butter or 1 × 15ml tbsp (1 tbsp) oil	6–8 min	turning 3–4 times
4 Cod portions in breadcrumbs	4–5 min	1 × 15ml tbsp (1 tbsp) oil	2–3 min	3–4 min
6 Fish fingers from frozen	5–6 min	Brush food with oil or melted butter	2 min	1–2 min
2 slices French toast	4–5 min	1 × 15ml tbsp (1 tbsp) oil	45 sec	45–60 sec
1 Pizza 17.5cm (7in), whole	3–4 min	15g ($\frac{1}{2}$oz) butter or 1 × 15ml tbsp (1 tbsp) oil	3–4 min	—
Oven chips 225g (8oz)	$3\frac{1}{2}$–4 min	—	$2\frac{1}{2}$–3 min	$2\frac{1}{2}$–3 min
2 Eggs	2–3 min	15g ($\frac{1}{2}$oz) butter or margarine (prick yolks)	$1\frac{1}{2}$–$1\frac{1}{4}$ min	—

using the browning dish so as to determine your personal preference. Try the minimum preheat time initially, but if you prefer browner meats then increase the time – to 6 minutes for smaller dishes and up to 8 minutes for the larger ones. Preheat time for vegetables is about 3–5 minutes, for breads about 2–4 minutes and eggs 1–2 minutes.

Placing a little oil or butter in the preheated dish immediately before adding the food improves the browning of many items, but in this case preheat the browning dish for 1 minute less than the normal time, then add the oil or butter.

Points to note

1 Do check with the instruction leaflet for your microwave cooker and be guided by the manufacturer's recommendations regarding the use of browning dishes in your particular model.

2 The feet on the base of the browning dish prevent it coming into direct contact with the oven shelf or a kitchen work surface but care should be taken when it is hot to ensure that the dish is not placed on a surface which could be damaged by the heat emanating from the underside.

3 The base of the browning dish becomes very hot,

so the use of oven gloves is advisable when handling the dish. While heating, the base of the dish will turn yellow but will return to its normal colour when cool.

4 The browning dish should not be preheated for longer than 6–8 minutes. IT IS NOT SUITABLE FOR USE IN A CONVENTIONAL OVEN OR ON A HOB.

5 The dish will require preheating again when cooking a second batch of food. Remove all excess food and drippings and preheat the dish for about half the original preheat time.

6 Turn the food over while there is still sufficient heat in the surface for browning the second side, but serve the food with the browned-first side face up.

7 To increase browning of the underside, flatten or press the food with a spatula to gain more contact with the base of the dish before placing it back in the microwave cooker.

8 While browning food, some smoke may be caused but this is quite normal. To help prevent splashings on to the oven interior cover the dish

A browning dish in use

with its lid or kitchen paper towel.

9 Do not attempt deep fat frying in the browning dish or in the microwave cooker at all as the temperature of the fat cannot be controlled.

10 Foods should be thawed before placing on the hot surface as any ice crystals present may prevent browning, although thinner foods – such as beefburgers or fish fingers – thaw out quickly during the cooking period.

11 The browning dish may be used as a casserole dish in the microwave cooker and is also useful for sautéeing vegetables such as onions and mushrooms.

12 The browning dish may be washed in a dishwasher or by hand but harsh abrasives must not be used as they may damage the special browning surface. Usually stubborn soilage can be softened by soaking. If necessary, mild cleaners or a plastic scouring pad may be used.

13 The preheat and cooking times given in the 'Browning Dish Chart' are intended only as a guide, as times vary depending on the size and shape of the dish, the output of the microwave cooker, the quantity of food being cooked and the degree of browning required. For those models with defrost control or variable power control, all preheating and cooking is carried out on 100% (Full) setting.

Microwave cooking techniques

Do not think that cooking by microwave means that you must learn completely new cooking techniques. Indeed, most of the basic rules still apply. It is just a case of adapting those rules and yourself to this new method of cooking food. Special points to watch for are given in the recipes but it is important to be aware of the factors which govern successful results.

Power of the oven and cooking times
Most microwave cookers have total power inputs of between 1,000 and 1,600 watts with outputs of between 500 and 700 watts respectively. The difference between the input and output power is used by the magnetron, stirrer blade, cooling fan, power converter and the interior and indicator lights.

It is the output power from the magnetron which controls the amount of microwave energy used in the oven cavity and the recipes in this book have been tested on microwave cookers with outputs of 650 watts. The instruction leaflet provided with your particular model should give details of the input and output power of the cooker, and timings on recipes should be adjusted accordingly. Cookers with lower outputs will require longer cooking times while higher outputs will need slightly shorter times. For example, a recommended cooking time of 10 minutes on 100% (Full) setting for a microwave cooker with a power output of 650 watts, would need to be adjusted to approximately 12–13 minutes for a 500 watt model and 8–9 minutes for a 700 watt cooker; shorter cooking times need less adjustment and longer times will require slightly more.

Density and texture
Because microwave cooking is so fast, differences in densities and textures will show up much more quickly in the end result. You will soon find out that a slice of light-textured French or Vienna bread will thaw and heat much more quickly than the sliced, prepacked variety and that a sponge cake will heat through faster than a meat pudding. This is because the lightness in the texture of the food allows the microwave energy to penetrate more easily.

Moisture
Moisture too can affect times as microwave energy reacts mainly on water molecules. Some of the recipes in this book have been adjusted to use more or less liquid than you are perhaps used to, in order to ensure successful results; for example, many vegetables can be cooked with very little water ensuring maximum flavour retention, whereas most cake mixtures have to be wetter than normal for a good even rise and a moist result.

Starting temperature
Differences in the temperature of the food when placed in the microwave cooker will affect the length of cooking time required. The colder the food, the longer the heating time, so allowances must be made when using food directly from the refrigerator or freezer.

Quantity
As the quantity of food placed into the oven is increased, the length of cooking time needs also to be increased proportionately. For example, one jacket potato weighing 100–150g (4–5oz) will take 5–6 minutes, two will take 7–9 minutes and three will take 10–11 minutes, and so on. A rough guide would be to allow approximately between one-third and one-half extra time when doubling the quantity of food to be heated. Similarly, if you use less than the quantities given in the recipes in this book, then the cooking times must be reduced accordingly.

Shape
The shape of the food should be as uniform as possible to obtain the best results, but of course this will not always be possible. To protect legs and wings of poultry or the thin ends of fish or a joint, such as a leg

of lamb, from overheating, it is quite in order to wrap them with a small smooth piece of tin foil, which will slow down the cooking of these sections of the food (see page 9). Generally, foods which have an overall longer, flatter surface area will heat more quickly than foods which are densely packed into a small dish.

Seasonings

Salt can have a toughening effect, especially on meat and poultry, so use minimal seasoning during the cooking process and, if in doubt, adjust the seasoning at the finish.

Standing time

It is always better to undercook than to overcook the food, giving a little extra time if required. However, foods do continue cooking after their removal from the oven and some food items will require this standing, resting or 'heat equalisation' period to assist with the general heating or cooking process.

When defrosting a joint, for example, it may begin to cook around the edges before thawing completely in the centre, thus a period of standing time in between periods of exposure to microwave energy is required to allow more even defrosting. Due to the continuation of the heating or cooking process during the standing time, it is possible to keep foods quite hot while further dishes are being cooked in the microwave. This is, of course, very useful when preparing a meal (see page 16). Some dishes – a cake or a pudding, for example – should be removed from the oven while the top is still slightly moist and left to stand until cooking is complete. Whether food is left to stand inside or outside the cooker is entirely up to you. It may be that you wish to leave the dish inside the oven out of the way, or you may have other food to cook in the meantime.

Turning and stirring

When food is placed into the oven cavity for heating, defrosting or cooking, microwave energy is directed into it from all directions including the base of the cavity beneath the glass shelf. However, due to the fact that microwaves penetrate the food only to a depth of 2.5cm (1in) it is quite likely that the entire outside surfaces of the food will heat through while the very centre remains relatively cool. The heating of the centre of the food relies on the conduction of heat through to this point, therefore the turning of the dishes or the stirring of some foods will be necessary during the heating process. The turning around of dishes means simply giving the dish a quarter turn (90°) or a half turn (180°) on the oven shelf. Turning dishes is not always necessary if you have a microwave cooker with a turntable.

Utensils

The shape of the dish will affect timings in the microwave; also some utensils will absorb more microwave energy than others. In the latter situation, the cooking times will be affected. This is explained more fully under the section 'Utensils' (page 6).

Covering the food

As, when cooking conventionally, lids on dishes or saucepans speed up the food heating process, so it is when cooking in the microwave. Whether a lid is placed on the casserole dish or the food is covered with clingfilm, steam is trapped inside and this will enable even and slightly faster results to be obtained. Covering food also allows minimal liquid to be used and ensures no flavour loss.

However, when heating through some items – crusty rolls or pastry dishes, for example – it would be undesirable to trap the steam as this would prevent a

crisp result. In these cases it would be preferable to cover the dish with a piece of kitchen paper towel which would assist in absorbing the moisture given off from the food.

Variable power control

The advantage of the variable power control featured on some models is that it enables a greater flexibility and control of the cooking speed. When a setting other than 100% (Full) has been selected on the variable power control, the microwave energy is automatically cycled on and off at varying rates depending on the setting chosen. At the lower setting the energy is off longer than it is on. As the control is moved to the higher settings the energy is on for longer periods and at 100% (Full) setting, the energy is on all of the time.

Choosing the setting is similar to selecting the oven temperature on your conventional cooker – the lower the setting or temperature, the longer the cooking time; the higher the setting, the shorter the cooking time. When a variable power setting has been selected, the timer does not stop and start, but continues to move while the energy switches on and off in the oven.

There are many different ways that manufacturers portray the variable power control settings on the control panels of their microwave cookers. Below are a few examples together with the approximate power (watts) outputs and percentage levels at those settings:

In addition, there are some electronic touch-control models available, where it is possible to obtain any percentage level you require to cook a particular dish just by selecting the appropriate figures.

It is important to understand the percentage outputs or power levels of your own microwave cooker and how these relate with the descriptions of the settings. This information should be given in the manufacturer's instructions to users.

By using the chart given below, it is possible to adapt the cooking times given in this book to suit your own particular model. However, the timings given in the chart are intended only as a guide for much depends on the shape, density, texture and temperature of the food. The calculations have been based on a microwave cooker with an average power output of 650 watts and, of course, this may vary between different models. Allow slightly extra time if using a microwave cooker with a lower output and slightly less time if using a cooker with a higher output.

Unless otherwise stated, the recipes in this book have microwave cooking times given for 100% (Full) setting. Some foods require slower cooking to help tenderise them, such as the less expensive cuts of meat. Slower cooking also allows food flavours to blend thoroughly, eg meat sauces and curries.

If you wish to slow down the heating or cooking cycle by using one of the lower settings on the variable power control, this chart will give you the approximate times for the other percentage outputs. Remember to check with your instruction booklet for the description of settings/power levels and the

1	2	3	4	5	6	7
KEEP WARM	SIMMER	STEW	DEFROST	BAKE	ROAST	HIGH
LOW	DEFROST	MED–LOW	MEDIUM	MED–HIGH	HIGH	FULL
150 WATTS	200 WATTS	250 WATTS	300 WATTS	400 WATTS	500 WATTS	650 WATTS
(25%)	(30%)	(40%)	(50%)	(60%)	(75%)	(100%)

Power levels *(cooking time in minutes)*

10%	20%	30%	40%	50% (defrost)	60%	70%	80%	90%	100% (full)
10	5	$3\frac{1}{4}$	$2\frac{1}{2}$	2	$1\frac{3}{4}$	$1\frac{1}{2}$	$1\frac{1}{4}$	1	1
20	10	7	5	4	$3\frac{1}{4}$	$2\frac{3}{4}$	$2\frac{1}{2}$	$2\frac{1}{4}$	2
30	15	10	$7\frac{1}{2}$	6	5	4	$3\frac{3}{4}$	$3\frac{1}{4}$	3
40	20	13	10	8	7	$5\frac{1}{4}$	5	$4\frac{3}{4}$	4
50	25	17	12	10	8	7	6	$5\frac{1}{2}$	5
60	30	20	15	12	10	8	$7\frac{1}{2}$	$6\frac{1}{2}$	6
70	35	23	17	14	12	$9\frac{1}{4}$	$8\frac{3}{4}$	$7\frac{3}{4}$	7
80	40	27	20	16	13	11	10	9	8
90	45	30	22	18	15	12	11	10	9
100	50	33	25	20	16	13	12	11	10

Seafood Flan (page 54)

percentage outputs of each one on your particular model. For times greater than 10 minutes, simply add together the figures in the appropriate column.

The following may be a useful guide as to the use of the variable power control percentage levels.

10–20% This low setting may be used for defrosting joints very slowly and for keeping foods warm for up to half an hour.

30–40% This setting is often used for defrosting, cooking less tender joints, slow-simmering cheaper cuts of meat, and for softening butter or cream cheese.

50–60% Use this setting for faster defrosting and simmering. It may also be used for defrosting and reheating frozen casseroles.

70–80% Most precooked foods and left-overs may be reheated using this setting. Use it also for roasting joints and for cooking foods which contain cheese or cream.

100% Use for bringing liquids to the boil and for preheating a browning dish. Most joints of meat and poultry, vegetables and fish can be cooked on this setting. However, many dishes may have a better flavour, texture and appearance if one of the slower settings is used, in which case a longer cooking period would be required. The variable power level time chart on page 14 will help you to calculate cooking times for different percentage levels.

Defrost control

It is when the microwave cooker is used in conjunction with the freezer that it really comes into its own. When defrosting food by microwave it is so fast compared with normal methods that there is less flavour loss and the risk of bacterial growth is minimal by comparison.

In some models, the defrost control may be incorporated as part of the variable power control (page 14) or it may be a separate switch or setting when the microwave cooker features just one or two different power levels.

Check with your instruction booklet for the percentage output of the defrost control as this may vary according to the model. The times given in this book are for a defrost control with 50% power level. Times should be adjusted accordingly for defrosting at higher or lower percentage outputs.

When the defrost control is operated, the microwave energy is cycled on and off in the oven to slow down the heating process. Otherwise, if frozen food were subjected to microwave energy until it was completely defrosted, the outer edges would begin to cook before the centre was thawed. Therefore, the defrost control allows the heat to equalise within the frozen food by gradual conduction and no surface cooking should take place.

Defrosting
When defrosting some foods – joints of meat or poultry, for example – additional standing periods are required to give a perfect thaw with no overheating of the outside edges. The food is then at an even temperature throughout, which ensures that when it is subsequently cooked, a good, even result is obtained. The number of heating and resting periods depends on the size or amount of food being defrosted, but generally the larger the item, the longer the periods of heating and of rest, with a final resting period being allowed before cooking or reheating.

Quicker defrosting is possible by simply placing frozen food into the microwave on defrost control until it is completely thawed, with one standing period halfway through; however, with this method less even results may be obtained. Alternatively, frozen food can be defrosted until it is warm to the touch on the outside edges and then left to stand at room temperature until it is completely thawed.

These defrosting methods are purely a matter of preference and time available and with experience you will be able to determine which method you prefer. You will also find that many items – vegetables, small cakes, rolls, bread slices, for example – may be thawed in a matter of seconds or minutes by using a 100% (Full) setting.

Most frozen foods should be placed into a suitable cooking container, first ensuring that it is large enough to hold the food once it has thawed – particularly important when defrosting soups, sauces, casseroles etc – and allowing sufficient room for stirring the food without spillage. Commercially frozen foods in foil trays or containers should be removed and placed into a dish suitable for microwave cooking.

Foods should be covered during the defrosting period where necessary. In the case of pastry dishes and bread, kitchen paper towels can be used to absorb any moisture. Small, smooth pieces of aluminium foil (page 9) will protect the narrower ends of poultry, meat or fish for part of the defrosting cycle to prevent any cooking of these thinner parts.

You can check whether food is defrosted either by feel or by using a thermometer (page 9); if it needs a little extra time, just put it back into the oven for a short while longer. It is important that meat and poultry are completely thawed and at an even

temperature throughout before cooking.

Defrosting and resting times are covered in more detail within the various recipe sections but the Convenience Foods Guide (page 20) deals with a range of commercially frozen foods and may be used as a general guide.

Heating and cooking
Some microwave cookers feature a defrost setting as the only alternative to 100% (Full) power level. In addition to using it for defrosting, the control may be used for heating and cooking those foods which benefit from a slower heating or cooking period:

1 Softening butter, melting method cake mixtures, melting chocolate, combining butter and sugar for caramelising, melting jellies, melting cheese.
2 Cooking casseroles, either when using tougher cuts of meat or when it is important that seasoning and spices blend well, eg curries.
3 Cooking tougher joints of meat.
4 Heating or cooking egg-based custards or cream sauces and setting the fillings in pre-baked flan cases, eg quiches.
5 Reheating larger casseroles thereby eliminating some of the need to stir as heating of the centre will be through conduction.
6 Cooking larger, flatter dishes to prevent the outsides drying out before the centre is cooked, eg cheesecake, bread pudding.
7 Poaching larger fruits, eg plums, greengages, peaches.
8 Warming bread or rolls in a basket.
9 Proving bread dough.
10 Poaching more delicate fish fillets or cutlets, eg salmon.

Whether you use the defrost control for some of the above items is a matter of choice. I have included some recipes for dishes which may be cooked on 50% (Defrost) setting, but if adapting your own recipes, allow approximately double the cooking time given for 100% (Full) setting and refer to the Power Level Chart on page 14.

Meal planning

A microwave oven will cook anything, in that it will turn food from the raw state into a cooked state. Through experience though I have found that some foods are better for being cooked conventionally. Yorkshire puddings and roast potatoes are good examples and, therefore, it makes sense if cooking a traditional Sunday lunch to cook the beef, potatoes and Yorkshire pudding in the normal way, leaving the microwave free for the vegetables, sauces, gravy and dessert. Foods which require deep fat frying must be cooked conventionally – eg fish in batter and chips. Frozen chips, however, can be thawed in the microwave while the fat is being heated conventionally and this will help to shorten the frying time.

Complete two-, three- or four-course meals can be cooked in the microwave with a little thought and planning. With experience, you will get more familiar with cooking and standing times. Dishes can be prepared in advance, so that they only need to be placed back in the oven to be reheated or to boost the serving temperature without any harm to the food or loss of flavour.

For many of us, Christmas lunch is possibly the most important meal of the year, with family and friends gathered together to enjoy this annual feast. Unfortunately, for the housewife, it could mean weeks of preparation culminating in her spending a great many hours slaving in a hot kitchen and consequently missing most of the festivities. With the aid of the microwave, Christmas lunch need not be a headache at all.

Most food items required for Christmas will freeze for a period of at least 3 months, so by the end of September food can be bought, prepared by microwave and frozen, then on the day it just needs to be defrosted and reheated. Many of the dishes required at Christmas are contained within the recipe section of the book. Do try the Christmas Pudding recipe (page 88) which really does save that day of 'steaming the puddings'.

A few tips

1 When first planning your menus cook each course separately, then gradually progress until a complete meal is cooked by microwave. You will find that organising a time plan will help.
2 As the microwave will not cook roast potatoes successfully, it is possible to roast potatoes and a joint together conventionally, leaving the microwave free for all the other items required.
3 Defrost all foods first, except vegetables which can be cooked from frozen. When a large number of vegetables are required, some may be partly cooked then left to stand while the rest are cooked.
4 When cooking a joint of meat or poultry, the vegetables should be cooked during its final standing time.
5 Try to serve one cold course – either a starter or sweet – which can be prepared by microwave then refrigerated.
6 Soups, casseroles, sauces and gravies may be prepared in advance, placed in serving dishes and then heated when required.

7 While eating one course, the next can be heating or cooking.
8 Where practicable, use clingfilm to cover dishes; also, use roasting bags which can be thrown away afterwards.
9 Line up in order all the the foods to be cooked in the microwave and clear the kitchen of any washing up.
10 Have aluminium foil ready so that you can wrap cooked items to keep them warm, or if there are a lot of dishes to be served, use the warming compartment in your conventional cooker.

Plate meals

With the microwave, you really can cook just once a day – an enormous help where members of the family require meals at different times. Whether refrigerated to reheat later or frozen to use next week, plate meals are ideal standbys for those members of the family who need to cook a meal for themselves when you are not there – and only one plate to wash up.

When arranging a meal on a plate for reheating, place the food within the well of the plate as evenly as possible; if thin slices of meat are to be served, it is better to place them in the very centre with the gravy poured over and the vegetables around. All items of food on the plate should be at the same temperature and cooked to the same degree to ensure evenness of reheating.

The plate should be covered with clingfilm whilst heating. The average plate meal (350–450g-/12–16oz) will take approximately 2–3 minutes to reheat from room temperature, 3–4 minutes from a refrigerator and 5–7 minutes from frozen. Allow about a minute standing time before uncovering and serving. If you are heating two plate meals, one after the other, pop the first one back after the second one has heated and give it an extra ½–1 minute to boost the temperature before serving.

Baby's food

Once prepared, baby's bottles and feeds may be quickly heated in the microwave, providing they are in a suitable microwave container. However, sterilisation of the bottles by microwave is not advised; it is generally recommended to sterilise by conventional methods.

Depending on the type of milk used, a 225ml (8oz) bottle feed should be heated for 45–60 seconds on 100% (Full) setting which will bring it to an even temperature for feeding. Similar heating times are required for baby's solid foods, although, of course, this will vary according to the type and quantity of the prepared foods.

Cleaning and care

The manufacturer's instruction leaflet supplied with your cooker will give detailed information on the cleaning and care of your particular model and should be read thoroughly. Any particular recommendations regarding the installation and siting of the appliance must be carefully followed.

Microwave cooking is clean because most dishes are covered while heating or cooking in the oven. In addition, with no radiant heat, the oven cavity remains relatively cool so that any splashing on the interior is normally easy to remove with a warm, soapy or just a damp cloth. Splashes which are more difficult to remove can be loosened by placing a cup of water in the oven and allowing it to boil for a few minutes. The steam will soften the soilage, which can then be wiped away more easily. Afterwards, rinse the surfaces and dry with a soft, dry cloth or kitchen paper towel. Any removable tray or oven shelf may be washed in the sink, dried and returned to the oven.

It is important that the oven cavity is kept clean for maximum efficiency. Soilage which is left in the oven will absorb microwave energy, slow down the cooking times and become more difficult to remove. Abrasive cleaning materials must not be used as they can scratch the interior surface finish. Condensation may occur during cooking some foods but providing it is wiped away with a dry cloth or kitchen paper towel afterwards, no harm should occur; alternatively, a piece of kitchen paper towel can be placed in the oven during cooking – this will assist by absorbing any moisture from the food.

The outside of the cabinet should be wiped with a damp cloth, dried and polished with a clean duster.

Ensure that any inlet or outlet air vents are kept clear of tea towels or cloths, etc during cooking processes.

Door seals must be kept clean and it is advisable to check periodically that the door hinges are not faulty or become rusty through neglect or lack of service. In the unlikely event of the glass or plastic front panel fracturing, do not use the cooker but contact your service engineer as soon as possible.

Useful information

The quantities for recipes in this book are given in metric and imperial measurements; in the following tables, American measurements are also given for comparison. Exact conversions do not always give acceptable working quantities and so the metric equivalents are rounded off into units of 25 grams. This may mean that the overall volume of the cooked product varies very slightly, but from experience I have found that this has little effect on the final result.

Measurement of ingredients

	Metric	Imperial
Weight	25g	1oz
Weigh and measure as	50g	2oz
accurately as possible and	75g	3oz
do not mix metric and	100g	4oz
imperial weights in one	150g	5oz
recipe as all measurements	175g	6oz
are proportionate.	200g	7oz
Imperial and American	225g	8oz
measurements in weight	250g	9oz
and length are the same	275g	10oz
	300g	11oz
	350g	12oz
	375g	13oz
	400g	14oz
	425g	15oz
	450g	16oz (1lb)
	475g	17oz
	500g ($\frac{1}{2}$kg)	18oz
	550g	19oz
	575g	20oz (1$\frac{1}{4}$lb)
Length	1.25cm	$\frac{1}{2}$in
	2.5cm	1in
	15.0cm	6in
	17.5cm	7in
	20.0cm	8in
	22.5cm	9in
	25.0cm	10in

	Metric	Imperial	American
Liquid	150ml	$\frac{1}{4}$pt	$\frac{2}{3}$ cup
Measurements in liquid	275ml	$\frac{1}{2}$pt	1$\frac{1}{4}$cups
and volume are different	425ml	$\frac{3}{4}$pt	2 cups
and these charts show the	550ml	1pt	2$\frac{1}{2}$ cups
equivalents using the	850ml	1$\frac{1}{2}$pt	3$\frac{3}{4}$ cups
American 8 ounce	1000ml (1l)	1$\frac{3}{4}$pt	4$\frac{1}{2}$ cups
measuring cup	1150ml	2pt	5 cups
Volume			
butter	225g	8oz	1 cup
sugar	225g	8oz	1 cup
flour	225g	8oz	2 cups
icing sugar	225g	8oz	1$\frac{1}{2}$ cups
rice	225g	8oz	1 cup
dried fruits	225g	8oz	1$\frac{1}{2}$ cups
breadcrumbs	225g	8oz	4 cups
grated cheese	225g	8oz	2 cups

	Metric	Imper-ial	Amer-ican
Spoon measures All spoon measures used in recipes throughout the book are level unless otherwise stated and are best used only for small quantities	5ml tsp 15ml tbsp 1½ × 15ml tbsp 2 × 15ml tbsp (or 30ml) 4 × 15ml tbsp (or 60ml)	1tsp 1tbsp 1½tbsp 2tbsp 4tbsp	1tsp 1tsbp 2tbsp 3tbsp 5tbsp

Courgettes Maison (page 39), Mushrooms à la Grecque (page 35), Creamy Haddock and Sweetcorn (page 35), Minestrone Soup (page 40) and Miniature Meatballs (page 39)

Conventional oven temperature chart

Oven temperatures		°C	°F	Gas
For those microwave users who wish to combine microwave and conventional cooking, this chart gives the comparative temperatures and settings between electric and gas ovens	VERY COOL	110 130	225 250	¼ ½
	COOL	140 150	275 300	1 2
	MODERATE	160 180	325 350	3 4
	MODERATE/ HOT	190/ 200	375/ 400	5/6
	HOT	220 230	425 450	7 8
	VERY HOT	240	475	9

Important points to remember

★ It is important to know all the features on your cooker and how they operate. Therefore, read the instruction leaflet before beginning to use the microwave cooker.

★ Do not switch on the oven when empty as this could damage the unit. A cup of water left in the unit when it is not being used for cooking will prevent damage in the event of the oven being switched on accidentally.

★ Care should be taken when removing dishes from the oven. Some dish materials absorb more microwave energy and may be hot to the touch. Heat transfer from foods to the dish may also make it hot to the touch and the use of oven gloves is advisable.

★ Deep fat frying must not be attempted as the temperature of the fat cannot be controlled.

★ When thawing frozen foods, remove any metal closures or ties before placing in the oven.

19

★ If food begins to 'pop' in the oven, it is an indication that foods may be overheating.

★ Some foods, eg casseroles, require stirring during defrosting, reheating or cooking to assist with the heating process.

★ When first using the microwave oven cook one type of food at a time, until you are able to judge the appearance of foods when cooking is complete.

★ After cooking with microwave energy, heat equalisation or standing time is recommended for some foods. This allows the distribution of heat evenly throughout the food.

★ Ensure that joints and poultry are completely thawed before cooking.

★ When reheating or cooking foods, best results are obtained if the food is at an even temperature throughout – particularly important when cooking foods after defrosting.

★ All the theory in this book regarding the use of ingredients when preparing food applies equally to both the conventional cooking method and the microwave method. It is only the quantities of those ingredients which may alter.

★ All cooking of the recipes given here is carried out in the microwave cooker using 100% (Full) power, unless otherwise stated.

★ The recommended cooking times are intended as a guide only as so much depends on the power input to the microwave oven cavity, the shape, material and size of the dish, the temperature of the food at the commencement of cooking and the depth of food in the dish.

★ If the quantities of food placed in the cooker are increased or decreased, then the cooking times must be adjusted accordingly.

★ Always undercook rather than overcook the food by cooking for a little less time than the recipe recommends, allowing the extra time if required.

★ Microwave cooking does not brown some food in the traditional way, but dishes can be finished off in a conventional oven or under a grill if you feel it is necessary.

★ Metal baking tins or metal trimmed dishes must NOT be used in the microwave cooker.

★ If the cooked or reheated food has become generally hard or dry, then overcooking or insufficient liquid content is indicated; remember to cook for a shorter period next time and check that the liquid measurements were correct.

★ Some microwave cooking instructions are given for models with variable power control settings, but it is still possible to cook the dish on models without this facility by referring to the Power Level Chart on page 14 and calculating the time required for cooking on 100% (Full) power. The automatic intermittent 'off' periods can be achieved manually by allowing the dish to rest at 1–2 minute intervals throughout the cooking duration.

★ Any warming or heating of food during the preparation of a dish is carried out in the microwave cooker and this information is given in the method for the recipe. In this way, you are using the microwave as a tool – to work for you in the kitchen. However, I have included, where appropriate, the alternative method of conventional cooking for those of you who may prefer traditional browning. Where I have suggested that a container is lined with clingfilm, this is for microwave cooking only. DO NOT line baking tins or dishes with clingfilm when cooking conventionally as it will melt; use lightly greased greaseproof paper instead.

Convenience foods guide

Not all convenience foods are included, but use this chart as a handy reference guide.

Food	Quantity	Method	Defrost time 50% (defrost)	Cook 100% (full)	Special points
CANNED FOODS Reheat Soup	275ml ($\frac{1}{2}$pt) 2 mugs or bowls	Pour into mug or soup bowl		3 min 5–6 min	Stir once during cooking
Pasta eg macaroni cheese	425g (15oz)	Place in bowl or serving plate, cover		4–5 min	Stir twice during cooking
Spaghetti in tomato sauce	440g (15$\frac{1}{2}$oz)	Place in bowl or serving plate, cover		3–4 min	Stir once during cooking

Food	Quantity	Method	Defrost time 50% (defrost)	Cook 100% (full)	Special points
Baked beans	220g (7¾oz)	Place in a bowl, or on a plate, cover		1–1½ min	Stir once during cooking
	425g (15oz)			3–4 min	
Peas or other small vegetables	425g (15oz)	Place in bowl, cover		4–4½ min	Stir twice during cooking
Custard or milk puddings	440g (15½oz)	Place in serving jug or bowl		3 min	Stir once during cooking
Sponge pudding	298g (10½oz)	Place in bowl or on a plate		2 min	Turn once during cooking
MEAT Reheat Cornish pasty	1	Stand on kitchen paper towel		¾–1½ min	Stand for 2–3 min before serving
Individual meat pie	1	Remove from foil tray, stand on kitchen paper towel		¾–1¼ min	Stand for 2–3 min before serving
Family size meat pie or quiche	450g (1lb)	Remove from foil dish and place on serving dish		6 min	Stand for 4 min halfway through and after cooking
4 Beefburgers, canned	283g (10oz)	Place on dish or serving plate, cover		4 min	Turn over halfway through cooking
Steak and kidney pudding, canned	440g (15½oz)	Remove from can, place in a bowl, cover		4–5 min	Stand for 5 min after cooking
Soya protein mince or chunks, canned	425g (15oz)	Place in a bowl, cover		3–4 min	Stir once during cooking
Frozen Roast meat in gravy	113g (4oz)		5 min, stand for 4 min	1½ min	Separate slices after defrosting
	340g (12oz)		10 min, stand for 9 min	3½ min	
Beefburgers	4	Place on kitchen paper towel		3–4 min	Turn over once during cooking
Shepherd's pie	454g (16oz)	Remove from foil dish and place on serving plate or dish	6 min, stand for 6 min 3 min, stand for 6 min	5–6 min	Turn once during cooking
Individual steak and kidney puddings	125g (5oz)	Remove from foil dish and place on serving plate	2 min, stand for 5 min 3 min, stand for 2 min	2½ min	Stand for 2 min before serving
Individual meals 'boil in bag'	227g (8oz)	Slit bag and place on serving plate	6 min, stand for 6 min	2–2½ min	Stand for 2 min before serving
Moussaka or Lasagne	454g (1lb)	Remove from foil dish and place on serving plate or dish, cover	8 min, stand for 6 min 4–5 min	9 min	Stand for 1 min before serving

Food	Quantity	Method	Defrost time 50% (defrost)	Cook 100% (full)	Special points
Sausage rolls (cooked)	1 4	Place on kitchen paper towel	30–60 sec, stand for 1 min 1½–2 min, stand for 3 min	15 sec 30–60 sec	
FROZEN FISH 2 Cod steaks	225g (8oz)	Place on plate or dish, cover	6 min, stand for 6 min	3 min	Turn over halfway through defrosting
'Boil in bag' fish, eg smoked haddock	198g (7oz)	Slit top of bag and place on plate	6 min, stand for 4 min	6 min	Separate fillets after defrosting
Fish steak in sauce 'boil in bag'	170g (6oz)	Slit top of bag and place on plate	4 min, stand for 4 min 2 min, stand for 5 min	1½ min	Shake contents of bag before serving
Fish fingers	10	Arrange in circle on plate	6 min, stand for 4 min	1½–2½ min	Dot with butter before cooking
2 Fish cakes	each 50g (2oz)	Place on plate	4 min, stand for 4 min	1–1½ min	Dot with butter before cooking
CAKES AND PUDDINGS Frozen Homemade cake	1 slice	Place on serving plate	1–2 min		Time varies with size and type of cake
Cream sponge	250g (10oz)	Place on serving plate	1–1½ min, stand until cream is completely thawed		Times given are sufficient to thaw the sponge only
Cream doughnut	1 4	Place on kitchen paper towel	30 sec, stand for 4 min 1¼ min, stand 5 min		
Jam doughnut	1 4	Place on kitchen paper towel	1½ min, stand 2 min 4 min, stand 4 min		
Cheesecake with fruit topping		Place on serving plate	4 min, stand 5 min 2 min, stand 5 min		
Reheat Mince pies, (cooked)	1 4	Place on kitchen paper towel		15 sec 1 min	Stand for 1–2 min before serving
Christmas pudding	1 whole 550–850ml (1–1½pt) 1 portion	In pudding basin On serving plate or dish		2–3 min 30–60 sec	Stand for 1 min before serving Stand for 1 min before serving
BREAD PRODUCTS Frozen Roll or large slice of bread	1 3	Place on kitchen paper towel or on oven shelf		10–25 sec 20–35 sec	Thawing time depends on density and type of bread

Small loaf	1	Place on oven shelf	4–5 min, stand for 8–10 min		
Large loaf	1		7–9 min, stand 12–16 min		
Pizza, large	1	Place on serving plate		5–6 min	
small	1			3 min	
MISCELLANEOUS Butter or margarine, frozen	250g (8.8oz)	Place in dish or plate, remove any foil wrapping	30–45 sec, stand 1 min 30 sec, stand 1 min		
Jelly	135g (4¾oz)	Break into cubes and place in bowl or measuring jug		15–30 sec	Stir well after heating and add remaining liquid quantity
Chocolate	100g (4oz)	Break into squares and place in bowl		1–1½ min	Beat well after melting
Toasted almonds	50g (2oz) blanched almonds	Place into boiling or roasting bag or on a plate		6 min or until toasted	Stir or shake frequently
Chestnuts	10–12	Slit the skins, place on plate		1–1½ min	Shell and use as required

Liver Pâté (page 35) and Quick Poor Man's Cassoulet (page 64)

Simple beginnings

This section is intended as a guide to help you to get to know your microwave cooker, starting off with some of the easier dishes and working towards more complicated ones. It will also assist you in getting familiar with cooking times and the appearance of foods when cooked by microwave. Recipes are included for drinks, snacks, egg and cheese dishes, all of which are easy to prepare so that members of your family will also be encouraged to start cooking by microwave.

Drinks

Preparing drinks in the microwave is quick and easy. It can even be used to reheat that forgotten half cup of tea or coffee or refresh left-over percolated or filtered ground coffee without loss of flavour. When making a milky drink in a mug or cup, just heat it until it is at a hot serving temperature; be careful not to let it boil over.

Snacks

Cooking 'something on toast' is simple with the microwave. Just make the toast conventionally, place it on the serving plate, cover with the prepared topping and cook in the microwave until hot. Alternatively, the topping may be heated in a separate bowl or dish and placed onto slices of hot buttered toast just before serving.

Hot chocolate or coffee (*for 1 cup*)
POWER LEVEL: 100% (FULL)

1–2 × 5ml tsp (1–2 tsp) drinking chocolate or instant coffee
sugar to taste, optional
175ml (6fl oz) milk or milk and water

1 Blend the chocolate or coffee with the sugar and a little of the liquid in a cup or mug.
2 Stir in the rest of the milk and heat for $1\frac{3}{4}$ min. Stir well before serving.

Note: *Heat 2 cups for 3 min.*

Tea (*for 1 cup*)
POWER LEVEL: 100% (FULL)

175ml (6fl oz) water
1 teabag
sugar and milk or lemon, to taste

1 Heat the water in a cup for 2 min.
2 Add the teabag and leave to 'brew' for 1 min.
3 Remove the teabag and add sugar and milk or lemon to taste.

Note: *Heat 2 cups for $3\frac{1}{2}$ min.*

Hot Bovril (*for 1 cup*)
POWER LEVEL: 100% (FULL)

175ml (6fl oz) water
1 × 5ml tsp (1 tsp) Bovril

1 Heat the water in a cup for 2 min.
2 Stir in the Bovril and serve straight away.

Note: *Heat 2 cups for $3\frac{1}{2}$ min.*

Egg nog (*serves 1*)
POWER LEVEL: 100% (FULL)

175ml (6fl oz) milk
1 egg
1 × 15ml tbsp (1 tbsp) sugar
grated nutmeg or few drops of vanilla essence

1 Heat the milk in a small jug, in the microwave, for $1\frac{1}{2}$ min.
2 Beat together the other ingredients. Whisk in the warm milk and serve.

DO NOT FREEZE

Hot apricot cider cup *makes about $1\frac{3}{4}$l ($2\frac{3}{4}$pt)*
POWER LEVEL: 100% (FULL)

1l ($1\frac{3}{4}$pt) strong cider
15cm (6in) cinnamon stick
15g ($\frac{1}{2}$oz) blanched almonds
1 × 822g (1lb 13oz) can apricots
2 × 241ml ($8\frac{1}{2}$fl oz) bottles tonic water

1 Heat 275ml ($\frac{1}{2}$pt) cider with the cinnamon and almonds in a large bowl for 5 min.

2 Blend the apricots and juice in a liquidiser or rub through a nylon sieve. Add the apricots to the hot liquid.

3 Add the remaining cider and the tonic water. Heat in the microwave for 10–15 min. Stir well and remove the cinnamon stick before serving.

DO NOT FREEZE

Mulled wine *makes about 1l (1¾pt)*
POWER LEVEL: 100% (FULL)
colour page 7

275ml (½pt) water
100g (4oz) sugar
4 cloves
7.5cm (3in) cinnamon stick
1 orange
1 lemon
1 bottle red wine
few lemon slices

1 Place the water, sugar and spices in a bowl and heat in the microwave for 4 min.

2 Slice the orange and lemon thinly and add to the spiced water. Leave to stand for 10 min.

3 Add the wine and reheat for 4 min. Strain the wine and heat for 2 min.

4 Garnish with extra lemon slices and serve hot.

DO NOT FREEZE

Spicy apple juice *makes about 700ml (1¼pt)*
POWER LEVEL: 100% (FULL)

450g (1lb) cooking apples
2 × 15ml tbsp (2 tbsp) water
sugar, to taste
150ml (¼pt) white wine
generous pinch cinnamon
275ml (½pt) cider

1 Place apples, water and sugar in a roasting bag, cover and cook in the microwave for 5 min.

2 Blend the apples with the white wine and cinnamon in a liquidiser or food processor.

3 Stir in the cider and serve – warm or cold.

DO NOT FREEZE

Porridge *(serves 1–2)*
POWER LEVEL: 100% (FULL)

4 × 15ml tbsp (4 tbsp) porridge oats
150ml (¼pt) water or milk and water
pinch salt
For serving:
sugar and milk or cream

1 Mix the porridge with the water (or milk and water) and salt in a serving bowl or dish.

2 Cook for 1¾ min, stirring twice throughout.

3 Allow to stand for 1–2 min.

4 Serve hot with sugar and milk or cream.

DO NOT FREEZE

Bacon sandwich *(serves 1)*
POWER LEVEL: 100% (FULL)

3 rashers bacon, trimmed
2 large slices bread
butter optional

1 Place the bacon rashers on a plate, cover with kitchen paper and cook for 2½–3 min.

2 Butter the bread slices or brush with the bacon fat.

3 Make up the sandwich and reheat for 30 sec; cut and serve.

Tomatoes on toast *(serves 1–2)*
POWER LEVEL: 100% (FULL)

4 tomatoes, cut into halves
salt and pepper
slivers butter
2 slices hot buttered toast

1 Place the tomato halves in a circle on a plate. Sprinkle with salt and pepper and add a sliver of butter to each half.

2 Cook for 3–4 min, turning the plate halfway through.

3 Serve on slices of hot buttered toast.

DO NOT FREEZE

Soft roe savoury *(serves 1–2)*
POWER LEVEL: 100% (FULL)

12 soft herring roes (about 100g/4oz)
25g (1oz) butter
salt, black pepper
chopped parsley
few drops lemon juice
2 slices hot buttered toast

1 Wash the roes and dry with kitchen paper.

2 Melt the butter in a shallow dish, in the microwave, for 1 min.

3 Add the roe, cover with a lid or clingfilm and cook for 1½ min.

4 Turn the roe and cook for a further 1 min. Season and add chopped parsley and lemon juice.

5 Serve on hot buttered toast.

DO NOT FREEZE

25

Baked beans or spaghetti on toast (*serves 1*)
POWER LEVEL: 100% (FULL)

1 slice hot buttered toast
3–4 × 15ml tbsp (3–4 tbsp) canned baked beans or spaghetti

1 Place the toast on a plate. Add the topping.
2 Heat through uncovered for $1\frac{1}{2}$–2 min. Serve immediately.

Note: *Alternatively, the topping can be heated separately in a dish or bowl for 1–$1\frac{1}{4}$ min before adding to the toast.*

DO NOT FREEZE

Cheese on toast (*serves 1*)
POWER LEVEL: 100% (FULL)

1 slice toast
thin slices cheese
chutney, sweet pickle or tomato slices, optional

1 Put the toast on a plate and cover with thin slices of cheese, making sure the layer of cheese is even.
2 Cook for 1–$1\frac{1}{4}$ min until the cheese is soft. Do not overheat otherwise the cheese will melt and run off the toast.
3 Top with chutney, sweet pickle or tomato slices and serve immediately.

DO NOT FREEZE

Mushrooms on toast (*serves 1–2*)
POWER LEVEL: 100% (FULL)

25g (1oz) butter
100g (4oz) button mushrooms, washed
salt and pepper
2 slices hot buttered toast

1 Melt the butter in a small bowl for 1 min. Add the mushrooms, tossing well in the butter.
2 Cover and cook for 2–$2\frac{1}{2}$ min. Serve on hot buttered toast.

DO NOT FREEZE

Sardines on toast (*serves 2–4*)
POWER LEVEL: 100% (FULL)

2 × 120g ($4\frac{1}{4}$oz) cans sardines
4 slices toast
butter, for spreading
2 tomatoes, sliced

1 Drain the sardines.
2 Butter the slices of toast and arrange the sardines on the toast.
3 Garnish each slice with pieces of tomato and heat one for 30–45 sec, or two for 1–$1\frac{1}{2}$ min, or four for $2\frac{1}{2}$–$3\frac{1}{2}$ min.

DO NOT FREEZE

Beefburgers and cheeseburgers (*makes 4*)
POWER LEVEL: 100% (FULL)
colour photograph opposite

4 beefburgers
4 baps or soft round rolls
butter
3–4 × 15ml tbsp (3–4 tbsp) fried onions, optional (page 76)
4 cheese slices, optional

1 Cook the beefburgers on a plate covered with a piece of kitchen paper, for $2\frac{1}{2}$–3 min.
2 Cut the rolls in half and spread with butter.
3 Place the onions, beefburgers and cheese slices in the rolls and heat through for $1\frac{1}{2}$–2 min.

Hot dogs (*makes 4*)
POWER LEVEL: 100% (FULL)

4 frankfurter sausages
butter
4 soft finger rolls
3–4 × 15ml tbsp (3–4 tbsp) fried onions (page 76)

1 Heat the frankfurters on a piece of kitchen paper for 1–$1\frac{1}{2}$ min.
2 Cut the rolls down one side and spread with butter.
3 Place the onions and sausages inside the rolls and reheat for 1–$1\frac{1}{2}$ min.

Jacket potatoes (*serves 2–4*)
POWER LEVEL: 100% (FULL)

2 potatoes (each 225–250g/8–9oz)
knob butter
salt and pepper

1 Scrub the potatoes then dry and prick them with a fork or score them.
2 Cook for 10–12 min, or until soft. Cut the potatoes in half and scoop out the soft potato.
3 Mix with the butter and seasoning, then pile the filling back into the potato skins. Reheat for $1\frac{1}{2}$ min before serving.

Variations: Add the following to the cooked potato and reheat as above.

Cheese
50g (2oz) cheese, grated
15g ($\frac{1}{2}$oz) butter
$\frac{1}{2}$ × 5ml tsp ($\frac{1}{2}$ tsp) milk

Bacon
50g (2oz) cooked bacon, chopped
$\frac{1}{2}$ × 5ml tsp ($\frac{1}{2}$ tsp) milk

Soured cream and chives
2 × 15ml tbsp (2 tbsp) soured cream
1 × 5ml tsp (1 tsp) chives, chopped

DO NOT FREEZE

Strawberry Jelly Mousse (page 88), Cheeseburgers (page 26), Toffee Mallow Crunch (page 100) and Double Deckers (page 97)

Sautéed kidneys on toast (*serves 1–2*)
POWER LEVEL: 100% (FULL)

4 lambs' kidneys
2 × 15ml tbsp (2 tbsp) seasoned flour
25g (1oz) butter
1 small onion, finely chopped
seasoning
2 slices hot buttered toast

1 Remove and discard the skin and cores from the kidneys. Chop finely and toss in the seasoned flour.
2 Melt the butter in a shallow dish for 1 min. Add the onion and cook for 1½ min.
3 Add the kidneys, stir, cover and cook for 4½ min stirring once during cooking.
4 Adjust seasoning and serve on hot buttered toast.

DO NOT FREEZE

Sausage, baked beans and mash (*serves 2*)
POWER LEVEL: 100% (FULL)

1 × 65g (2½oz) medium-sized packet instant potato
275ml (½pt) water
4 large sausages
4–6 × 15ml tbsp (4–6 tbsp) baked beans

1 Place the potato in a small bowl. Heat the water in the microwave for 3 min. Pour over the potato.
2 While the potato is standing, cook the sausages. First prick them well, then cover with kitchen paper. Cook for 4–5 min, turning once.
3 Cover and heat the baked beans in a bowl for 2–2½ min, stirring once halfway through.
4 Reheat the potato for 1 min and serve hot with the sausages and baked beans.

DO NOT FREEZE

Quick crumpet pizzas
POWER LEVEL: 100% (FULL)

Ingredients for each pizza:
1 crumpet
knob butter
½ slice cooked ham
2 thin slices tomato
pinch mixed herbs
salt and pepper
few onion rings
15–25g (½–1oz) cheese, grated
For garnish: sliced green olives

1 Heat the crumpet in the microwave until hot (½–1½ min depending on quantity).
2 Lightly butter the crumpet. Place the ham on the crumpet and top with tomato, herbs, seasoning, onion and grated cheese.
3 Cook as follows:
   1 crumpet – 1 min
   2 crumpets – 1½ min
   4 crumpets – 2½ min
   or until the cheese is melted.
4 Garnish with sliced green olives.

DO NOT FREEZE

Tuna-stuffed rolls (*serves* 4)
POWER LEVEL: 100% (FULL)

4 crispy rolls
25g (1oz) butter
1 × 198g (7oz) can tuna fish, flaked
50g (2oz) cheese, finely grated
salt and pepper

1 Slice the tops from the rolls, remove the centres from the rolls and crumb.
2 Melt the butter in a bowl for 1 min, add the breadcrumbs, tuna fish, cheese and seasoning. Mix well together and heat through for 1–1½ min.
3 Fill the rolls with the mixture, replace tops and heat through for 1–1½ min.
4 Serve warm.

Sausage and egg crisp (*serves* 4–6)
POWER LEVEL: 100% (FULL) or 75%

1 medium onion, grated or finely chopped
450g (1lb) sausagemeat
1 × 15ml tbsp (1 tbsp) mixed dried herbs
50g (2oz) white breadcrumbs
2 eggs, beaten
milk for mixing
salt and pepper
60–75g (2½–3oz) potato crisps

1 Mix the onion with the sausagemeat, herbs and breadcrumbs.

2 Stir in the eggs and sufficient milk to form a soft mixture. Add seasonings to taste.
3 Place the mixture in a 17.5–20cm (7–8in) shallow dish. Smooth the top and cover.
4 Cook for 4 min on 100% (full) setting. Allow to rest for 4 min, turn the dish and cook for a further 4–5 min. Alternatively cook on 75% setting for 10–12 min, turning 2–3 times.
5 Drain off any fat. Crumble the potato crisps and scatter over the top of the sausagemeat.
6 Heat for 1 min and serve immediately.

DO NOT FREEZE

Corned beef hash (*serves* 4–6)
POWER LEVEL: 100% (FULL)

A substantial supper dish.

25g (1oz) butter or margarine
1 large onion, peeled and finely chopped
225g (8oz) can corned beef
450g (1lb) potatoes, cooked
225g (8oz) can baked beans
salt and freshly ground black pepper
½–1 × 5ml tsp (½–1 tsp) worcestershire sauce
paprika pepper for sprinkling, optional

1 Melt the butter or margarine in a large pie dish for 1 min, toss in the onion, cover and cook for 4–5 min until soft and transparent.
2 Dice the corned beef and potato. Add the corned beef and half the potato to the onion with the baked beans, seasonings and worcestershire sauce. Mix well together and smooth the top. Scatter the remaining potato over the top.
3 Cover and cook for 3–4 min until heated through.
4 Brown the potato under a grill or sprinkle with paprika pepper. Serve hot.

Eggs and cheese
When 'frying' or poaching eggs in the microwave, prick the yolks with a sharp pointed knife otherwise steam build-up may cause them to explode; for the same reason, never boil eggs in their shells in the microwave, except by the method given in this section. The cooking times given for eggs are intended as a guide as much depends on how well done you like them, but remember to remove them from the oven just before they are set as they will carry on cooking for a short while afterwards. Leave them to stand for a minute before serving but if they are not set sufficiently for your liking, return them to the oven for a further 10–15 seconds. Be careful not to overcook eggs as they may become rubbery in texture.

DO NOT FREEZE ANY OF THE EGG DISHES

Cheese melts very quickly in the microwave, so remove cheese dishes from the oven just as the cheese is softened; if overcooked, cheese becomes leathery.

Boiled eggs (*serves 2–4*)
POWER LEVEL: 100% (FULL)

While this recipe does not save cooking time, it is the only method by which eggs may be boiled in the microwave cooker.

4 eggs
boiling water

1 Wrap the eggs tightly in pieces of smooth foil to reflect the microwave energy and thus prevent the eggs from exploding.
2 Place the eggs in a bowl and just cover with boiling water.
3 Cover and cook for 3–4 min, stand for 2 min.
4 Drain and unwrap the eggs and serve straight away.

Poached eggs (*serves 2–4*)
POWER LEVEL: 100% (FULL) AND 50% (DEFROST)

boiling water
4 eggs
4 slices hot buttered toast

1 Pour the boiling water into individual cups, ramekin dishes or small bowls to a depth of about 2.5cm (1in).
2 Place the dishes in a circle in the microwave and heat on 100% (full) setting until boiling. Carefully break the eggs into each dish and prick the yolks.
3 Cook on 50% (defrost) setting for 3–3½ min, until the whites are set, turning the dishes halfway through.
4 Serve on hot buttered toast.

Note: *Cook 1 egg on 50% (defrost) setting for 1–1½ min, 2 eggs for 1½–2 min.*

Scrambled eggs (*serves 2*)
POWER LEVEL: 100% (FULL)

4 eggs
4 × 15ml tbsp (4 tbsp) milk
pinch salt
25g (1oz) butter
2 slices hot buttered toast

1 Beat the eggs, milk and salt together.
2 Melt the butter in a bowl for 1 min. Pour in the egg mixture and cook for 1 min.
3 Stir well and cook for 2–2½ min, stirring every 30 sec. Serve with hot buttered toast.

Note: *Halve the above cooking times for 2 scrambled eggs.*

Baked eggs (*serves 1–2*)
POWER LEVEL: 50% (DEFROST)

butter or margarine
2 eggs

1 Lightly grease 2 small dishes or bowls with the butter or margarine.
2 Break the eggs into the dishes and prick the yolks.
3 Cover and cook for 2–2½ min, turning the dishes once halfway through.

Note: *Baked eggs may be used in place of hardboiled eggs when required chopped for use in salads or fillings.*

Fried eggs (*serves 1–2*)
POWER LEVEL: 100% (FULL)

15g (½oz) butter or margarine
2 eggs

1 Melt the butter in 2 small shallow dishes or saucers. Break the eggs into the hot butter and pierce the yolks.
2 Cover and cook for 30 sec. Stand for 1 min, then turn the dishes and cook for 15–30 sec.

Egg and bacon (*serves 1*)
POWER LEVEL: 100% (FULL)

2 rashers bacon
1 egg

1 Lay the bacon in a shallow dish, cover with kitchen paper and cook for 1 min.
2 Remove the bacon and add the egg. Pierce the yolk, cover and cook for 30 sec.
3 Stand for 1 min, return the bacon to the dish and cook, still covered, for 15–30 sec.

Baked egg custard (*serves 4–5*)
POWER LEVEL: 100% (FULL) AND 50% (DEFROST)

425ml (¾pt) milk
3 eggs, lightly beaten
50g (2oz) sugar
few drops vanilla essence
ground nutmeg for sprinkling

1 Heat the milk in a measuring jug or bowl for 3 min on 100% (full) setting. Add the eggs, sugar and vanilla essence and whisk lightly.
2 Strain and pour the mixture into individual bowls or ramekin dishes. Sprinkle with nutmeg and cover.
3 Arrange in a circle in the microwave and cook on 50% (defrost) setting for 10–12 min, turning the dishes halfway through. If not quite set, allow an extra 1–2 min, or leave to stand.
4 Serve warm or leave to chill in the refrigerator.

DO NOT FREEZE

Herb omelette (*serves 1–2*)
POWER LEVEL: 100% (FULL)

15g (½oz) butter
4 eggs
2 × 15ml tbsp (2 tbsp) milk
salt and pepper
1 × 15ml tbsp (1 tbsp) mixed dried herbs

1 Melt the butter in a 20cm (8in) shallow dish for 30 sec. Mix all the other ingredients together in a separate bowl.
2 Brush the melted butter around the base and sides of the dish. Pour in the egg mixture.
3 Cover and cook for 1 min, stir gently, cook for 1 min. Uncover and cook for 1 min. Turn out of the dish and serve immediately.

Variations
Any of the following ingredients can be substituted in place of the herbs. Cook as above.

2 × 15ml tbsp (2 tbsp) cheese, grated
2 × 15ml tbsp (2 tbsp) cooked ham, chopped
2 × 15ml tbsp (2 tbsp) cooked onion, chopped.

Eggs florentine (*serves 2*)
POWER LEVEL: 100% (FULL) AND 50% (DEFROST)

450g (1lb) spinach, washed
15g (½oz) butter
salt and pepper
2 eggs
150ml (¼pt) cheese sauce (page 46)
25g (1oz) cheese, grated
paprika pepper for sprinkling

1 Cook the spinach with just the water that clings to its leaves in a covered dish or boiling bag for 6–8 min on 100% (full) setting. Leave to stand for a few minutes. Drain well, chop roughly and stir in the butter and seasoning. Place in a dish and keep warm.
2 Poach the eggs in small dishes (page 29) on 50% (defrost) setting for 1½–2 min. Leave to stand for 30 sec.
3 Drain the eggs and place them on top of the spinach. Coat with the cheese sauce and sprinkle with the grated cheese and paprika pepper.
4 Reheat the dish on 100% (full) setting for 30–60 sec or brown the top under a hot grill.
5 Serve straight away.

DO NOT FREEZE

Piperade (*serves 4*)
POWER LEVEL: 100% (FULL)

3 × 15ml tbsp (3 tbsp) cooking oil
2 medium onions, peeled and finely sliced
2 cloves garlic, crushed
2 red peppers, deseeded and sliced
4 tomatoes, skinned
4 eggs
salt and freshly ground black pepper
For serving:
triangles fried or toasted bread or
fresh bread and butter

1 Heat the oil in a large bowl or dish for 1½ min. Add the onions and garlic, cover and cook for 3 min. Add the peppers and continue to cook for 3 min.
2 Chop the tomatoes and add them to the onions and peppers. Season lightly, cover and cook for a further 3–4 min until the vegetables are tender, stirring occasionally.
3 Whisk the eggs lightly in a bowl and pour over the vegetables; stir lightly as for scrambled eggs, cover and cook for 1 min, stir then cook for a further 1–2 min. When the eggs begin to thicken, the piperade is cooked.
4 Serve immediately with triangles of fried or toasted bread, or with plenty of fresh bread and butter.

DO NOT FREEZE

Macaroni cheese (*serves 3–4*)
POWER LEVEL: 100% (FULL)

100g (4oz) macaroni
275ml (½pt) boiling water
1 × 15ml tbsp (1 tbsp) oil
1 × 5ml tsp (1 tsp) salt
1 small onion, chopped
pinch salt
25g (1oz) butter
25g (1oz) plain flour
425ml (¾pt) milk
1 egg yolk
75g (3oz) cheddar cheese, grated
salt and freshly ground black pepper
For garnish:
tomato, sliced

1 Place the macaroni in a large, shallow dish. Pour over the boiling water and stir in the oil and salt. Cook for 10 min, then separate with a fork.
2 Place the onion and a pinch of salt in a roasting bag and cook for 3 min.
3 Melt the butter in a bowl for 1 min. Blend in the flour and gradually stir in the milk. cook for 5–6 min, stirring every minute. Beat in the egg yolk, cheese, seasoning and cooked onion.
4 Pour the sauce over the macaroni and mix well.
5 Cook for 3 min and serve immediately, garnished with the sliced tomato. Alternatively sprinkle with a little extra grated cheese and brown the top under a hot grill.

Individual cheese soufflés (serves 8)

POWER LEVEL: 100% (FULL)

25g (1oz) butter
15g (½oz) flour
150ml (¼pt) milk
75g (3oz) cheese, finely grated
3 eggs, separated
seasoning
paprika pepper for sprinkling

1 Place the butter in a bowl and melt for 1 min.
2 Stir in the flour and gradually blend in the milk. Cook for 1½ min until thickened, stirring every 30 sec. Add the cheese.
3 Beat the egg yolks into the mixture one at a time then add seasoning.
4 Whisk the egg whites until stiff, fold into the mixture and divide between 8 individual soufflé dishes or ramekin dishes.
5 Cook 4 at a time for 1–1½ min. Serve immediately, sprinkled with a little paprika pepper.

DO NOT FREEZE

Cheesy Spinach Flan (page 34) and Rich Fruit Cake (page 97)

Spanish omelette (serves 2)

POWER LEVEL: 100% (FULL) AND 50% (DEFROST)

100g (4oz) frozen mixed vegetables
1 cooked potato, chopped
1 tomato, chopped
1 × 15ml tbsp (1 tbsp) oil
4 eggs
seasoning

1 Place the vegetables and tomato in a shallow dish with the oil. Cover and cook on 100% (full) setting for 1½–2 min.
2 Whisk the eggs and seasoning together and pour over the vegetables. Cook uncovered on 50% (defrost) setting for 8 min.
3 Leave to stand for 1 min.
4 Do not fold the omelette but serve on a warm plate with a green salad.

31

Eggs en cocotte (*serves 4*)
POWER LEVEL: 50% (DEFROST)

150ml ($\frac{1}{4}$pt) double cream
salt and pepper
garlic salt
paprika pepper
25g (1oz) butter
4 eggs
For garnish:
parsley sprigs

1 Mix the cream with the seasonings, to taste. Whip the mixture lightly until the cream is thick but not stiff.
2 Divide the butter between 4 ramekin or individual soufflé dishes and melt for 1 min. Brush the butter around the dishes and break an egg into each dish.
3 Pierce the yolk of each egg, then spoon over the cream mixture.
4 Cover and cook for 2–2$\frac{1}{2}$ min and stand for 1 min.
5 Sprinkle with more paprika and garnish with parsley before serving.

DO NOT FREEZE

Welsh rarebit (*serves 1–2*)
POWER LEVEL: 100% (FULL)

100g (4 oz) cheddar cheese, grated
25g (1oz) butter
1 × 5ml tsp (1 tsp) dry mustard
1 × 15ml tbsp (1 tbsp) brown ale
salt and pepper
2 slices toast

1 Place the ingredients for the topping in a small bowl and cook for 20 sec. Stir well.
2 Spoon the topping on to the slices of toast and cook for 15–30 sec. Serve immediately.

DO NOT FREEZE

Swiss toast (*serves 2–4*)
POWER LEVEL: 100% (FULL)

4 slices toast
butter
4 slices cooked ham
4 slices swiss cheese
For serving:
scrambled eggs (page 29)

1 Butter the toast, put a slice of ham on each and cover with a slice of cheese.
2 Cook, one slice at a time, for 1–1$\frac{1}{4}$ min.
3 Serve with scrambled egg.

DO NOT FREEZE

Flan case: rich shortcrust pastry *for a 20cm (8in) flan case*
POWER LEVEL: 100% (FULL)

175g (6oz) plain flour
pinch salt
75g (3oz) butter or margarine
2 × 5ml tsp (2tsp) caster sugar, optional
1 egg yolk
2 × 15ml tbsp (2 tbsp) water

1 Sift the flour with the salt and rub in the butter or margarine finely. Stir in the sugar if using.
2 Beat the egg yolk with the water and add to the flour. Mix well, then knead together lightly.
3 Chill before rolling out.

To line a flan dish
Roll out the pastry into a circle 5cm (2in) larger than the dish. Wrap the pastry loosely around the rolling pin and lift into the flan dish. Ease the pastry into shape removing any air from under the base, pressing well into the sides and taking care not to stretch the pastry. Cut the pastry away but leave 6mm ($\frac{1}{4}$in) above the rim of the flan dish. Carefully ease this down into the dish, or flute the edges and leave slightly higher than the rim of the dish (this allows a little extra height to the sides of the flan case to compensate for any shrinkage during cooking). Alternatively, run the rolling pin across the top of the flan to cut off surplus pastry. Prick the base well.

To bake blind
Using a long, smooth strip of aluminium foil measuring approximately 3.75cm (1$\frac{1}{2}$in) wide, line the inside, upright edge of the pastry flan case to protect this section from overcooking in the microwave. Place two pieces of absorbent kitchen paper over the base, easing around the edge and pressing gently into the corner between base and side to help keep the foil strip in position. Place in the microwave and cook on 100% (full) setting for 4–4$\frac{1}{2}$ min, giving the dish a quarter turn every minute. Remove the kitchen paper and foil and cook for a further 1–2 min.

Alternative conventional bake
Line the pastry flan case with a circle of lightly greased greaseproof paper (greased side down) or kitchen paper. Half fill the paper with uncooked beans, lentils, small pasta or rice which may be specially kept for this purpose. Alternatively, line the pastry flan case with foil only. Cook in a preheated oven at 200°C (400°F) Mark 6 for 15–20 min, until the pastry is nearly cooked. Remove the lining and bake for 5–10 min until the base is firm and dry.

Light wholemeal pastry
Half the plain flour is replaced by wholemeal flour.

Sweet rich shortcrust pastry
If preferred, 2 × 5ml tsp (2 tsp) caster sugar may be added to the crumb mixture before adding the egg. This gives a sweeter pastry for dishes with sweet fillings.

Cheese and onion flan (*serves 6*)
POWER LEVEL: 100% (FULL)

225g (8oz) light wholemeal pastry (page 32)
25g (1oz) butter or margarine
450g (1lb) onions, peeled and finely sliced
175g (6oz) strong cheddar cheese, grated
salt and freshly ground black pepper
paprika pepper for sprinkling

1 Roll out the pastry, line a 20cm (8in) flan dish and bake blind (page 32). Reserve the trimmings.
2 Melt the butter in a large bowl for 1 min. Add the onions and toss well in the butter.
3 Cover and cook for 8–9 min until soft, shaking or stirring twice throughout.
4 Add the cheese to the onions with the salt and black pepper. Mix well together and place into the flan case.
5 Roll out the trimmings from the pastry and cut into thin strips. Lay the strips of pastry over the filling in a lattice style.
6 Cook for 3 min, rest for 3 min. Turn the dish and cook for a further 2–3 min or until lattice is cooked and set.
7 Leave to stand for a few minutes and then sprinkle with paprika pepper.
8 Serve hot or cold as a snack or part of a main course.

Fondue (*serves 4*)
POWER LEVEL: 100% (FULL) OR 50% (DEFROST)
colour page 7

1 clove garlic, crushed
100g (4oz) gruyère cheese, grated
100g (4oz) emmenthal cheese, grated
black pepper
grated nutmeg
175–225ml (6–8fl oz) dry white wine
squeeze of lemon juice
2 × 5ml tsp (2 tsp) cornflour
1 liqueur glass kirsch
For serving:
crusty bread

1 Rub the garlic round the inside of a heatproof dish. Place the cheese, seasonings, wine and lemon juice in the dish.
2 Melt the cheese in the microwave for 4–5 min on 100% (full) setting. (The cheese and wine will not combine at this stage.)
3 Blend the cornflour with the kirsch, add to the fondue, stir and cook on 100% (full) setting for 1–2 min until slightly thickened.
4 Serve with crusty bread, keeping the fondue warm over a spirit lamp or dish warmer.

Note: *In models with a 50% (defrost) control, the fondue can be cooked as follows: Melt the cheese mixture on 50% (defrost) setting for 10 min, add the blended cornflour and kirsch, then cook on 50% (defrost) for 6 min.*

DO NOT FREEZE

Cheesy spinach flan (serves 4–6)
POWER LEVEL: 100% (FULL) AND 50% (DEFROST)
colour page 31

1 17.5cm (7in) baked flan case (page 32)
For the filling:
1 small onion, peeled and chopped
225g (8oz) cream cheese
2 egg yolks
225g (8oz) cooked fresh or frozen spinach, chopped
salt and pepper

1 Place the onion in a small dish, cover with clingfilm or a lid and cook on 100% (full) setting for 2 min.
2 Cream the cheese until soft, then add the egg yolks, beating well together.
3 Stir in the onion and spinach then season to taste.
4 Spoon the mixture into the precooked flan case and cook on 50% (defrost) setting for 12–14 min until the filling is set.
5 Serve hot or cold.

Cheese and ham au gratin (serves 4)
POWER LEVEL: 100% (FULL) AND 50% (DEFROST)

25g (1oz) butter or margarine
1 medium onion, peeled and chopped
2 cloves garlic, crushed or finely chopped
100g (4oz) ham, cut into strips
2 eggs, beaten
275ml ($\frac{1}{2}$pt) milk
100g (4 oz) emmenthal or gruyère cheese, grated
salt and freshly ground black pepper
pinch nutmeg
450g (1lb) potatoes
25g (1oz) parmesan cheese, grated
paprika pepper for sprinkling

1 Lightly grease a shallow ovenware or au gratin dish.
2 On 100% (full) setting, melt the butter or margarine for 1 min in a bowl, add the onion and garlic, toss well in the fat and cook for 3–4 min. Add the ham and cook for 1$\frac{1}{2}$ min.
3 Add the eggs to the milk with threequarters of the cheese, seasoning and nutmeg. Stir into the onions and ham.
4 Peel and coarsely grate the potatoes, squeeze and drain off any liquid. Add to the egg mixture. Mix well and pour into the greased dish.
5 Cover and cook on 50% (defrost) setting for 18–20 min, turning every 5 min, until cooked and set.
6 Sprinkle with the remaining cheese, the parmesan cheese and paprika pepper.
7 Cook on 100% (full) setting for 1–1$\frac{1}{2}$ min until the cheese is melted.
8 Serve hot with crusty french bread.

Cheese pudding (serves 4)
POWER LEVEL: 100% (FULL)

6 medium slices brown bread
25g (1oz) butter
150ml ($\frac{1}{4}$pt) milk
2 eggs, beaten
150ml ($\frac{1}{4}$pt) dry white wine
salt and freshly ground black pepper
100g (4oz) cheese, grated
paprika pepper for sprinkling

1 Lightly grease a 15–17.5cm (6–7in) soufflé dish.
2 Remove the crusts from the bread, cut into dice and place in the greased dish.
3 Add the butter to the milk and warm for 2 min. Stir until the butter is melted.
4 Beat the eggs with the butter and milk, add the wine and season well. Pour over the bread.
5 Sprinkle over the cheese and paprika pepper.
6 Cook for 4–5 min, turning every 2 min.
7 Serve immediately.

DO NOT FREEZE

Cheese potato pie (serves 2–4)
POWER LEVEL: 100% (FULL)

450g (1lb) potatoes, peeled
2 × 5ml tsp (2 tsp) salt
boiling water
175g (6oz) cheese
1 small onion, peeled
salt and freshly ground black pepper
25g (1oz) butter
paprika pepper for sprinkling

1 Lightly grease an ovenware dish.
2 Slice the potatoes thinly. The slices must be very thin so use a vegetable slicer or pare with a vegetable peeler.
3 Rinse the potatoes well, place in a bowl, sprinkle with salt and just cover with boiling water. Heat in the microwave until the potatoes are transparent and soft. Drain.
4 Grate the cheese and the onion. Arrange overlapping layer of potatoes in the bottom of the prepared dish, sprinkle with salt and pepper, grated onion, dot with butter and sprinkle with cheese. Continue the layers, alternating the potatoes with the cheese and onion, finishing with a layer of cheese.
5 Cover and cook for 6–8 min. Sprinkle with paprika and serve hot.

Starters

The recipes in this section include a variety of appetising hot and cold dishes. They make excellent starters to a meal but some may also be used for snacks or supper dishes. Most of them can be prepared in advance and refrigerated until required; those to be served hot can be quickly reheated when you and your guests are ready.

Mushrooms à la grecque (serves 6)

POWER LEVEL: 100% (FULL)
colour page 19

2 × 15ml tbsp (2 tbsp) olive oil
1 small onion, peeled and finely chopped
1 clove garlic, crushed
450g (1lb) button mushrooms, sliced
4 tomatoes, skinned and deseeded
salt and freshly ground black pepper
1 × 15ml tbsp (1 tbsp) tomato purée
1 wine glass white wine
2 × 15ml tbsp (2 tbsp) chopped parsley

1 Place the oil in a large serving dish with the onion and garlic. Cover and cook for 2 min.
2 Add the mushrooms, tomatoes, salt and freshly ground black pepper, cover and cook for 3 min.
3 Blend the tomato purée and wine together and add to the mushrooms. Stir, cover and cook for $2\frac{1}{2}$ min.
4 Stir half the parsley into the dish and allow to cool, then chill for 2 hrs.
5 Serve cold, sprinkled with the rest of the parsley.

Liver pâté (serves 8–12)

POWER LEVEL: 50% (DEFROST)
colour page 23

350g (12oz) lamb's liver
50g (2oz) chicken livers
1 slice bread
1 small onion, peeled
100g (4oz) pork fat
$\frac{1}{2}$ × 5ml tsp ($\frac{1}{2}$ tsp) garlic salt
$\frac{1}{2}$ × 5ml tsp ($\frac{1}{2}$ tsp) ground black pepper
1 × 5ml tsp (1 tsp) mixed herbs
1 × 5ml tsp (1 tsp) lemon juice
1 egg
75ml (3fl oz) red wine

For garnish:
gherkin, tomato, juniper berries or olives
For serving:
hot toast

1 Mince the livers, bread, onion and pork fat. Stir in all the other ingredients.
2 Grease a suitable deep round dish. Pile the pâté mixture into the dish and press down firmly.
3 Cover and cook on 50% (defrost) setting for 10 min, stand for 5 min, cook for 5 min. Allow to cool slightly, then cover and place weights on top of the pâté. Leave in the refrigerator overnight.
4 Turn out and garnish before serving with hot toast.

Creamy haddock and sweetcorn (serves 4)

POWER LEVEL: 100% (FULL)
colour page 19

450g (1lb) potatoes, creamed (page 76) or
1 medium-sized packet instant potato
knob butter
1 × 15ml tbsp (1 tbsp) chopped parsley
20g ($\frac{3}{4}$oz) butter
20g ($\frac{3}{4}$oz) plain flour
175ml (6fl oz) milk
225g (8oz) haddock, cooked and flaked
50g (2oz) frozen sweetcorn
salt and pepper
2 × 15ml tbsp (2 tbsp) single cream
paprika pepper for sprinkling

1 Cook and mash the potatoes or make up the instant potato. Mix in a large knob of butter and the parsley. Using a large rosette pipe, pipe a border of potato onto 4 scallop shells.
2 Place butter, flour and milk in a bowl. Cook for 1 min, beat thoroughly, cook for 1 min. Repeat this operation until the sauce thickens (about 3 times).
3 Add the fish and corn to the sauce and season to taste. Cook for 1 min, stir, cook for 1 min. Add the cream, adjust the seasoning and spoon the mixture into the scallop shells.
4 Heat the scallops for 4–5 min. Sprinkle with paprika and serve immediately.

DO NOT FREEZE

Quick kipper pâté *(serves 4)*
POWER LEVEL: 100% (FULL)

1 × 175g (6oz) pkt frozen kipper fillets
100ml (4fl oz) natural yoghurt
1 small onion, chopped
salt and pepper
squeeze lemon juice
1 × 15ml tbsp (1 tbsp) chopped parsley
For garnish:
parsley sprigs
For serving:
buttered toast

1 Slit the kipper bag. Heat the kippers for 2 min, stand for 5 min.
2 Cook the kippers for 3 min. Skin the fillets and flake the fish. Place in a liquidiser goblet or food processor. Blend until well mixed.
3 Cook the onion in a small, covered dish for 1½–2 min, then add to the kipper mixture. Add the other ingredients – seasoning to taste.
4 Pack the mixture into a serving dish and garnish with parsley. Cover and chill in the refrigerator for at least an hour before serving. Serve with hot buttered toast.

DO NOT FREEZE

Artichokes with vinaigrette dressing *(serves 4)*
POWER LEVEL: 100% (FULL)

An excellent starter when you have time to linger over a meal.

4 medium globe artichokes
150ml (¼pt) salted water
2 × 15ml tbsp (2 tbsp) lemon juice
For the vinaigrette dressing:
150ml (¼pt) oil
3 × 15ml tbsp (3 tbsp) wine vinegar
salt and freshly ground black pepper
1 × 15ml tbsp (1 tbsp) chopped fresh herbs

1 Wash the artichokes and trim off the lower leaves if necessary.
2 Place in a large roasting bag or covered casserole dish with the salted water and lemon juice. Cook for 15–20 min, turning the dish or rearranging the artichokes twice throughout. Test whether cooked by removing one of the leaves – it should pull away quite easily. Drain and leave to cool.
3 Blend the oil, vinegar and seasoning by whisking together in a bowl or placing in a screw-top jar and shaking vigorously. Alternatively, blend in a

Globe Artichokes (above) with Hollandaise Sauce (page 48)

liquidiser. Beat in the chopped herbs.

4 Serve the artichokes on individual dishes or plates, pour over a little dressing and hand the rest separately.

Note: *The artichokes may also be served hot with hollandaise sauce (page 48) or with melted butter.*

DO NOT FREEZE THE VINAIGRETTE DRESSING

Melon with port jelly *(serves 4)*
POWER LEVEL: 100% (FULL)
colour photograph above

A really delicious, refreshing but simple starter.

1 lemon table jelly to make 550ml (1pt)
150ml ($\frac{1}{4}$pt) water
2 × 15ml tbsp (2tbsp) redcurrant jelly
2.5cm (1in) cinnamon stick
275ml ($\frac{1}{2}$pt) port, approximately
2 small melons
For serving: crushed ice and mint or lemon

Melon with Port Jelly (below)

1 Break up the lemon table jelly into a bowl or measuring jug. Add the water, redcurrant jelly and the cinnamon stick. Stir well.
2 Heat for about 1–1$\frac{1}{2}$ min, then stir until the jelly cubes are dissolved. Make up to 550ml (1pt) with the port and allow to cool
3 Cut the melons in half, and remove a thin slice of the peel from the base of each half so that it will stand firm. Remove the seeds.
4 When the jelly is nearly cold, strain through a sieve and divide between the four halves of melon. Refrigerate until the jellies are set.
5 Serve on beds of crushed ice on individual serving plates or dishes. Garnish with sprigs of mint or lemon twists.

Note: *If there is any jelly left over, allow it to set, chop finely, and pile it up in the centre of the melon halves.*

DO NOT FREEZE

Baked stuffed tomatoes (*serves 6*)
POWER LEVEL: 100% (FULL)
colour page 73

12 large, firm tomatoes
40g (1½oz) butter or margarine
1 onion, peeled and finely chopped
175g (6oz) cooked meat, minced
100g (4oz) cooked rice
1 × 15ml tbsp (1 tbsp) single cream or top of the milk
2 × 5ml tsp (2 tsp) worcestershire sauce
2 × 15ml tbsp (2 tbsp) chopped parsley
salt and freshly ground black pepper
50g (2oz) cheese, grated
1 × 15ml tbsp (1 tbsp) fresh breadcrumbs
For garnish:
parsley sprigs

1 Cut a thin slice from the top of each tomato and scoop out the flesh.
2 Melt the butter or margarine in a bowl for 1½ min, toss in the onion and cook for 3–4 min.
3 Stir in the meat, rice, cream or top of the milk, worcestershire sauce and the chopped parsley. Season to taste.
4 Fill the tomato cases with the meat mixture and place in a shallow, round serving dish.
5 Cover and cook for 4–5 min until heated through.
6 Mix together the cheese and breadcrumbs and sprinkle over the top of the tomatoes. Cook uncovered for 1½–2 min until the cheese has melted.
7 Serve hot, garnished with parsley sprigs.

Potted shrimps (*serves 4*)
POWER LEVEL: 100% (FULL)

225g (8oz) frozen shrimps (or prawns)
225g (8oz) unsalted or clarified butter
½ × 5ml tsp (½ tsp) dried basil
pepper to taste
For garnish:
parsley sprigs and lemon slices

1 Put the shrimps in a bowl, cover and heat in the microwave for 30 sec. Stand for 1 min, then heat for 1 min.
2 Place about 150g (5oz) of butter in a bowl and melt for 3 min. Liquidise or blend the shrimps, melted butter and seasonings to give a smooth paste.
3 Press mixture firmly into a small dish and chill for ½ hr.
4 Melt the remaining butter for 2 min. Smooth the top of the shrimp mixture and pour over the butter. Cover and leave to chill in the refrigerator.
5 Serve garnished with parsley sprigs and lemon slices.

DO NOT FREEZE

Chinese cucumber starter (*serves 4*)
POWER LEVEL: 100% (FULL)
colour page 45

1 large cucumber, washed
40g (1½oz) butter
100g (4oz) button mushrooms, washed
1 × 5ml tsp (1 tsp) cornflour
75ml (2½fl oz) chicken stock
75ml (2½fl oz) single cream
few drops soy sauce
100g (4oz) shelled prawns
For garnish:
freshly chopped chives or dill
lemon or cucumber twists

1 Cut the cucumber into 1.25cm (½in) dice, place in a dish, cover and cook for 3 min. Drain.
2 Melt the butter in a bowl for 1–1½ min, add the mushrooms, cover and cook for 2 min. Add the cucumber and cook for 3 min until the vegetables are tender but crisp.
3 Blend the cornflour with the stock, add the cream and soy sauce. Pour over the vegetables and heat for 1–2 min. Stir in the prawns and continue to heat for 1–2 min.
4 Divide the mixture between 4 individual serving dishes and garnish with the chopped herbs and lemon or cucumber twists.
5 Serve hot.

Note: *Tiny, button mushrooms are best but if the mushrooms are large, cut into slices before cooking.*

DO NOT FREEZE

Hot cinnamon grapefruit (*serves 2*)
POWER LEVEL: 100% (FULL)

1 large grapefruit
pinch cinnamon
25g (1oz) demerara sugar
2 × 15ml tbsp (2 tbsp) sherry or rum, optional
1 glacé cherry

1 Halve the grapefruit, remove the pips and loosen around the flesh of the fruit. Place each half grapefruit in an individual bowl.
2 Mix the cinnamon and sugar together. If using the sherry or rum, pour 1 × 15ml tbsp (1 tbsp) over each half grapefruit, then sprinkle with the sugar mixture. Place half a glacé cherry in the centre of each half grapefruit.
3 Heat the grapefruit halves in the microwave for 1–1½ min, turn, heat for 1–1½ min. Serve immediately.

DO NOT FREEZE

Miniature meatballs (*makes about 40*)

POWER LEVEL: 100% (FULL)
colour page 19

100g (4oz) butter, softened
1 × 15ml tbsp (1 tbsp) onion, finely chopped
3 cloves garlic, finely chopped
2 × 15ml tbsp (2 tbsp) chopped parsley
pinch pepper
1 onion, finely chopped
450g (1lb) minced beef
50g (2oz) breadcrumbs
salt and pepper
1 egg, beaten
1 × 15ml tbsp (1 tbsp) tomato purée
1 × 5ml tsp (1 tsp) worcestershire sauce
For garnish:
chopped parsley

1 Prepare garlic butter by blending the first five ingredients thoroughly. Cover and chill until hard.
2 Place the onion in a large bowl and cook for 1½ min. Add the other ingredients and mix thoroughly.
3 Shape about 1 × 15ml tbsp (1 tbsp) meat mixture around ¼ × 5ml tsp (¼ tsp) of garlic butter, sealing in the butter completely.
4 Place the meatballs in a single layer in the serving dish 12–18 at a time. Cook uncovered for 3 min, turn the dish, cook for 2 min.
5 Garnish with extra chopped parsley, before serving.

Courgettes maison (*serves 4 or 8*)

POWER LEVEL: 100% (FULL) AND 50% (DEFROST)
colour page 19

8 small courgettes, trimmed and washed
25g (1oz) butter
1 onion, finely chopped
4 tomatoes, skinned
1 × 5ml tsp (1 tsp) paprika pepper
salt and freshly ground black pepper
225g (8oz) shelled prawns
275ml (½pt) béchamel sauce (page 46)
50g (2oz) parmesan cheese, grated
paprika pepper for sprinkling

1 Place the courgettes in a large dish, cover and cook on 100% (full) setting for 4–5 min. Rinse in cold water.
2 Cutting lengthways, remove a thin slice from the top of each courgette. Discard the slices. Scoop out the flesh from each courgette and chop finely.
3 Melt the butter in a bowl for 1 min on 100% (full) setting. Add the onion, cover and cook for a further 2 min.

4 Remove the seeds from the tomatoes, chop the flesh and add to the onions with the flesh from the courgettes, paprika pepper and seasonings. Cover and cook on 100% (full) setting for 3 min.
5 Stir the prawns into the mixture and divide between the courgette cases.
6 Cover the dish and cook on 100% (full) setting for a further 3–4 min.
7 Mix the béchamel sauce with half the cheese and spoon over the courgettes. Sprinkle the remaining cheese and paprika pepper over the top of the sauce.
8 Cook, uncovered, for 5 min on 50% (defrost) setting until heated through.

FREEZE THE SAUCE SEPARATELY. FINISH AND GARNISH JUST BEFORE SERVING

Baked avocados with walnut cheese (*serves 4*)

POWER LEVEL: 100% (FULL)
colour page 65

This is an unusual way of serving avocado pears as a starter and makes a change from the normal 'vinaigrette' or 'with prawns'.

2 avocado pears, ripe
few drops lemon juice
50g (2oz) butter
100g (4oz) cream cheese
50g (2oz) walnuts
freshly ground black pepper
For serving:
lemon wedges

1 Cut the avocados in half, remove the stones and sprinkle each half with a little lemon juice.
2 Place the avocado halves in a microwave dish with the narrow ends towards the centre. Cover with a lid or clingfilm slit with the pointed end of a sharp knife.
3 Place in the microwave and cook for 5–7 min until soft, depending on the ripeness of the pears. Allow to stand for a few minutes. (The avocado flesh will darken slightly during the cooking process).
4 Meanwhile, cream the butter and cheese together until light. Reserving 4 walnut halves, chop the remainder very finely and mix into the creamed butter and cheese. Add freshly ground black pepper to taste.
5 Uncover the avocados and divide the walnut and cheese mixture between the 4 halves. Heat for 1 min – just long enough to warm the topping.
6 Add a walnut half to each avocado and serve hot with lemon wedges.

DO NOT FREEZE

Soups

Whether used as a starter to a meal or as a snack, home-made soups are nourishing and always welcome. They may be quickly prepared in the microwave and frozen in individual portions if required, so that if every member of the family prefers different soups, well why not? An individual bowl or mug of soup may be quickly heated in the microwave in 3 minutes and two will take about 5 minutes. Shop-bought soups can be prepared in the microwave on 100% (full) setting as follows:

Canned condensed soups

Add hot water and whisk thoroughly before heating in a large jug or dish; the 275g (10oz) size will take about 6–7 minutes to come to boiling point. Stir thoroughly halfway through the cooking time and whisk well before serving.

Packet soups

Empty the soup into a large jug or bowl and stir in the recommended amount of cold water. Allow to stand for 20–30 minutes to allow the ingredients to soften. Cover and bring to the boil in the microwave. Depending on the quantity of soup this will take 8–10 minutes on 100% (full) setting. Cook for 1–2 minutes, stir well and leave to stand for 5 minutes before serving.

Minestrone soup (serves 4–6)
POWER LEVEL: 100% (FULL)
colour page 19

25g (1oz) butter
1 carrot, peeled and diced
1 onion, peeled and finely chopped
1 small leek, finely sliced
1 stick celery, finely chopped
1 clove garlic, finely chopped
550ml (1pt) boiling chicken stock
15g ($\frac{1}{2}$oz) long-grain rice
salt and pepper
225g (8oz) tomatoes, skinned and chopped
2 × 15ml tbsp (2 tbsp) baked beans
For garnish:
1 × 5ml tsp (1 tsp) chopped parsley
For serving:
grated parmesan cheese

1 Melt the butter in a large bowl for 1 min. Add the carrot, onion, leek, celery and garlic. Toss well in the butter, cover and cook for 3 min.
2 Add boiling stock, rice and seasoning. Cover and cook for 5–6 min, stirring once halfway through.
3 Add the tomatoes and baked beans and continue to cook, covered, for a further 5–6 min.
4 Sprinkle with parsley and serve with grated parmesan cheese.

Greek lemon soup (serves 4)
POWER LEVEL: 100% (FULL)
colour photograph opposite

1l (1$\frac{3}{4}$pt) jellied chicken stock
4 × 15ml tbsp (4 tbsp) cooked rice
2 eggs
1 lemon, grated rind and juice
salt and freshly ground black pepper
For garnish:
a little finely grated lemon rind

1 Heat the chicken stock in a large bowl until boiling, about 8–10 min. Add the rice.
2 Beat the eggs with the lemon rind and juice and seasoning.
3 Add a little of the hot stock to the eggs, beating well until smooth and then pour the mixture back into the stock, stirring continuously.
4 Heat without boiling for approximately 2–3 min, whisking every 15 sec to incorporate the egg mixture thoroughly into the stock.
5 Adjust seasoning and serve hot sprinkled with a little finely grated lemon rind.

Chilled avocado soup (serves 4)
POWER LEVEL: 100% (FULL)

Serve as a first course for a special luncheon menu.

15g ($\frac{1}{2}$oz) butter
1 small onion, peeled and finely chopped
1 large avocado pear, ripe
1 × 15ml tbsp (1 tbsp) lemon juice
150ml ($\frac{1}{4}$pt) chicken stock
150ml ($\frac{1}{4}$pt) milk
150ml ($\frac{1}{4}$pt) double cream
salt and freshly ground black pepper
a little green food colouring, optional

1 Melt the butter in a large dish for 30 sec. Add the onion, cover and cook for 3 min until soft.
2 Halve the avocado pear, remove the stone and scoop out the flesh with a spoon. Add to the onion with the lemon juice and mix together until blended.
3 Add chicken stock, milk and half the cream. Purée in a liquidiser or blender or pass through a sieve. Add seasoning and the colouring if desired.
4 Chill thoroughly and just before serving swirl in the remainder of the double cream.
5 Serve with melba toast.

DO NOT FREEZE WITH THE RESERVED CREAM. SWIRL IN THE CREAM JUST BEFORE SERVING

Borsch (*serves 4–6*)
POWER LEVEL: 100% (FULL)

This beetroot soup can be served hot or cold, with soured cream swirled over the top to give a good colour contrast.

1 onion, peeled and finely chopped
1 large carrot, peeled and finely chopped
2–3 parsley sprigs

Greek Lemon Soup (page 40) and Stuffed Cabbage Leaves (page 74)

1 bay leaf
salt and freshly ground black pepper
1l (1¾pt) boiling chicken stock
450g (1lb) cooked beetroot, chopped
150ml (¼pt) soured cream
For garnish:
Chopped chives or mint

1 Place the onion, carrot, herbs, seasoning and boiling stock in a large serving dish. Cover and cook for 5 min.
2 Add the beetroot and cook for 10 min.
3 Purée the soup in a blender, then strain through a sieve into the serving dish.
4 Wipe the edges of the dish, stir in the soured cream and serve hot. If serving cold, chill in the refrigerator and stir in the cream just before serving.
5 Serve sprinkled with chopped chives or mint.

DO NOT FREEZE WITH THE SOURED CREAM. FINISH AND GARNISH JUST BEFORE SERVING

Cream of cucumber soup (serves 4–6)
POWER LEVEL: 100% (FULL)

25g (1oz) butter or margarine
1 onion, peeled and sliced
850ml (1½pt) boiling chicken stock
1 large cucumber, peeled and roughly chopped
1 mint sprig
salt and pepper
2 × 5ml tsp (2 tsp) cornflour
150ml (¼pt) double, single or soured cream
a few drops green food colouring, optional
For garnish:
diced cucumber or chopped mint

1 Melt the butter in a large bowl for 1 min, add the onion and toss well in the butter. Cover and cook for 2 min.
2 Add the stock, cucumber, mint and seasoning. Cover and cook for 30 min. Remove the mint.
3 Purée the soup in a blender or pass through a sieve.
4 Blend the cornflour with a little of the soup, then add it to the rest and cook for 3–4 min until it thickens.
5 Adjust the seasoning and stir in the cream. Add a few drops of green colouring if desired.
6 Serve hot or very cold garnished with cucumber or chopped mint.

DO NOT FREEZE WITH THE CREAM. FINISH AND GARNISH JUST BEFORE SERVING

Vichyssoise soup (serves 4)
POWER LEVEL: 100% (FULL)

675g (1½lb) leeks, washed and trimmed
225g (8oz) potatoes, peeled
40g (1½oz) butter
1 stick celery, finely sliced
550ml (1pt) boiling chicken stock
salt and pepper
550ml (1pt) milk
275ml (½pt) double cream
freshly grated nutmeg

1 Slice the leeks finely and cut the potatoes into small dice.
2 Melt the butter for 1½ min, add the leeks, potatoes and celery. Mix well together, cover and cook for 5–6 min.
3 Pour on the boiling chicken stock, add salt and pepper. Cover and cook for 12–14 min, until the vegetables are tender.
4 Blend the mixture in a liquidiser or pass through a sieve.
5 Add the milk, cover and cook for 5–6 min until heated through.
6 Allow to cool, check seasoning and stir in the cream.
7 Serve chilled, sprinkled with freshly grated nutmeg.

DO NOT FREEZE WITH THE CREAM. FINISH JUST BEFORE SERVING

Cream of chicken and sweetcorn soup
(serves 4)
POWER LEVEL: 100% (FULL)

1 × 15ml tbsp (1 tbsp) oil
1 onion, peeled and finely chopped
1 stick celery, chopped
425ml (¾pt) boiling chicken stock
225g (8oz) sweetcorn kernels, fresh or frozen
salt and pepper
100g (4oz) cooked chicken, diced
150ml (¼pt) milk
3 × 15ml tbsp (3 tbsp) single cream or top of the milk
25g (1oz) flaked almonds, toasted

1 Heat the oil in a large bowl for 1–2 min, add the onion and celery, cover and cook for 3 min.

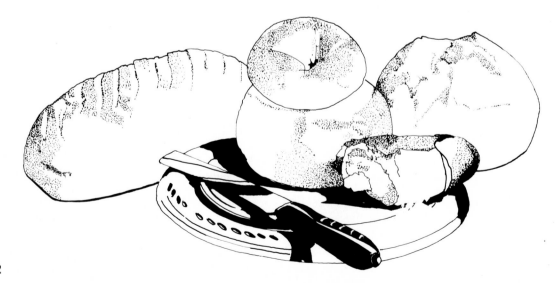

2 Add the chicken stock, sweetcorn and seasonings and cook for 5 min. Add chicken and cook for 2 min.

3 Blend the soup with the milk in a liquidiser or pass through a sieve. Reheat the soup for 2 min.

4 Stir in the cream and serve sprinkled with the flaked almonds.

Note: *If preferred, the soup may be served without puréeing. Use 550ml (1pt) boiling chicken stock and omit the milk. Thicken the soup with 2 × 5ml tsp (2 tsp) arrowroot mixed with a little water, then stir in the cream or top of the milk. Mix the almonds into the soup before serving.*

DO NOT FREEZE WITH THE CREAM. FINISH AND GARNISH JUST BEFORE SERVING

French onion soup (*serves 4*)
POWER LEVEL: 100% (FULL)

50g (2oz) butter
450g (1lb) onions, peeled and thinly sliced
25g (1oz) flour
salt and freshly ground black pepper
1 × 5ml tsp (1 tsp) sugar
550ml (1pt) boiling beef stock
For serving:
4 slices french bread, toasted
grated cheese

1 Heat the butter in a large, shallow serving dish for 2 min. Toss the onion in the butter and cook for 5 min.

2 Add the flour and mix into the butter and onion. Add salt and pepper to taste and the sugar.

3 Add the stock gradually, mix well together. Cover and cook for 25 min.

4 Place the toasted bread on top of the soup and sprinkle with the grated cheese.

5 Heat in the microwave for 2–3 min until the cheese is melted, or alternatively brown the cheese under a hot grill.

6 Serve immediately.

Note: *For a 'special' soup, 2 × 15ml tbsp (2 tbsp) brandy may be added to the cooked soup before garnishing with the toast and cheese.*

DO NOT FREEZE WITH THE TOAST, ADD WITH THE CHEESE JUST BEFORE SERVING

Celery and pea soup (*serves 4–6*)
POWER LEVEL: 100% (FULL)

1 onion, peeled and chopped
$\frac{1}{2}$ head celery, trimmed and roughly chopped
225g (8oz) frozen peas
550ml (1pt) boiling chicken stock
salt and pepper
1 bay leaf
bouquet garni
1 × 15ml tbsp (1 tbsp) cornflour
150ml ($\frac{1}{4}$pt) milk
150ml ($\frac{1}{4}$pt) single cream
For garnish:
freshly chopped parsley

1 Place the onion, celery, peas and stock into a large casserole dish or bowl. Add salt and pepper, bay leaf and bouquet garni.

2 Cover and cook for 12–15 min until the vegetables are tender.

3 Remove bay leaf and bouquet garni. Blend the soup in a liquidiser or pass through a sieve.

4 Blend the cornflour with the milk and then add to the soup in the bowl. Heat for 3–4 min or until slightly thickened and boiling.

5 Stir in the cream to give a swirled effect and serve sprinkled with chopped parsley.

DO NOT FREEZE WITH THE CREAM. FINISH AND GARNISH JUST BEFORE SERVING

Cream of turnip soup (*serves 6*)
POWER LEVEL: 100% (FULL)

Use early turnips for this delicious vegetable soup.

50g (2oz) butter
350g (12oz) young turnips, peeled and diced
225g (8oz) potatoes, peeled and diced
1 leek, trimmed, washed and chopped
1 onion, peeled and chopped
25g (1oz) flour
2l ($3\frac{1}{2}$pt) boiling chicken or vegetable stock
salt and freshly ground black pepper
2 egg yolks
3 × 15ml tbsp (3 tbsp) double cream
For garnish:
croûtons

1 Melt the butter in a large bowl for $1\frac{1}{2}$–2 min. Add all the vegetables, toss well in the butter. Cover and cook for 12–15 min, shaking or stirring every 5 min.

2 Stir in the flour and blend in the boiling stock. Season to taste.

3 Cook for 15–20 min until the vegetables are tender. Purée the soup in a liquidiser or pass through a sieve.

4 Beat the egg yolks with the cream, add a little of the soup and stir until well blended. Add this to the soup and mix well. Adjust seasoning.

5 Heat without boiling. Serve hot, garnished with croûtons or hand them separately.

DO NOT FREEZE

Sauces

At first glance you may think that it is hardly worth cooking sauces in the microwave as the time saved is negligible. However, providing the mixture is stirred at intervals during the heating stage, the result is a very smooth sauce and the advantage is that other ingredients can be added for heating or cooking during or after the sauce has cooked, and of course there will be only one dish or bowl to wash.

When heating dishes which have a sauce as part of the main ingredient, ie au gratin dishes, always use a lower 50–70% setting otherwise the sauce will be bubbling and overcooking before the rest of the food is heated through.

Apple sauce *makes about 275ml ($\frac{1}{2}$pt)*
POWER LEVEL: 100% (FULL)

450g (1lb) cooking apples
15g ($\frac{1}{2}$oz) butter
sugar, to taste
1 strip lemon peel
1 × 15ml tbsp (1 tbsp) water

1 Peel and core the apples and slice thinly. Cook with the other ingredients in a covered dish or roasting bag for 6 min.
2 When cooked, remove lemon peel, beat well, purée in a blender or sieve.
3 Serve hot or cold with rich meat or poultry, eg pork or duck.

Butterscotch sauce *makes about 150ml ($\frac{1}{4}$pt)*
POWER LEVEL: 100% (FULL) AND 50% (DEFROST)
colour photograph opposite

50g (2oz) light, soft brown sugar
50g (2oz) butter
2 × 15ml tbsp (2 tbsp) golden syrup
15g ($\frac{1}{2}$oz) chopped almonds, optional
squeeze lemon juice

1 Heat the sugar in a bowl on 100% (full) setting for 30 sec. Add the butter and syrup.
2 Heat on 50% (defrost) setting for 1 min, then stir thoroughly adding almonds and lemon juice.
3 Heat on 50% (defrost) setting for 3–4 min, stirring every minute, or until sugar dissolves.

Note: *Use as a topping for ice-cream and desserts.*

Jam sauce *makes about 425ml ($\frac{3}{4}$pt)*
POWER LEVEL: 100% (FULL)

275ml ($\frac{1}{2}$pt) water or fruit juice
225g (8oz) jam
1 × 15ml tbsp (1 tbsp) cornflour or arrowroot
4 × 15ml tbsp (4 tbsp) cold water
lemon juice

1 Warm the water or fruit juice for 2–2$\frac{1}{2}$ min and stir in the jam.
2 Blend the cornflour or arrowroot with the cold water and stir into the jam. Cook for 2–3 min, stirring every minute.
3 Add lemon juice to taste.

Syrup sauce
Follow the ingredients and method for jam sauce substituting syrup for the jam.

Chocolate sauce *makes about 425ml ($\frac{3}{4}$pt)*
POWER LEVEL: 100% (FULL)
colour photograph opposite

175g (6oz) plain chocolate
1 × 5ml tsp (1 tsp) butter
3–4 × 15ml tbsp (3–4 tbsp) golden syrup
1 × 5ml tsp (1 tsp) coffee essence
150ml ($\frac{1}{4}$pt) single cream

1 Break up the chocolate and place in a bowl with the butter, golden syrup and coffee essence.
2 Heat until melted 2–3 min, stirring once halfway through.
3 Stir in the single cream and heat without boiling.
4 Serve hot or cold.

Chocolate Sauce (above) and Butterscotch Sauce (above)

Chinese Cucumber Starter (page 38) and Fennel Sauce (page 46)

Savoury white sauce *makes about 275ml ($\frac{1}{2}$pt)*
POWER LEVEL: 100% (FULL)

25g (1oz) butter
25g (1oz) plain flour
275ml ($\frac{1}{2}$pt) milk
salt and pepper

1 Melt the butter in a medium-sized glass bowl for 1–1$\frac{1}{2}$ min. Blend in the flour and gradually stir in the milk.
2 Add the seasonings and cook for 4–5 min, stirring every minute. Use as required.

Variations
One of the following ingredients may be added to the sauce 2 min before the end of the cooking time:

Prawn sauce: 100g (4oz) peeled prawns
Cheese sauce: 50–75g (2–3oz) cheese, grated (*colour page 80*)
Mushroom sauce: 50g (2oz) mushrooms, chopped
Onion sauce: 100g (4oz) cooked onion, chopped
Parsley sauce: 2 × 5ml tsp (2 tsp) parsley, chopped
Egg sauce: 1 hard-boiled egg, chopped finely

White wine sauce

Follow the recipe replacing a wine glass of dry white wine for the same measure of milk.

Fennel sauce (*serves 4*)
POWER LEVEL: 100% (FULL)
colour page 45

This sauce makes a good accompaniment to salmon or mackerel.

1 medium head fennel, washed and trimmed
2 × 15ml tbsp (2 tbsp) salted water
For the sauce:
15g ($\frac{1}{2}$oz) butter
15g ($\frac{1}{2}$oz) flour
salt and pepper
275ml ($\frac{1}{2}$pt) milk and fennel juice, mixed
3 × 15ml tbsp (3 tbsp) single cream

1 Cut the fennel into small pieces and cook with the salted water in a covered dish or boiling bag for 6–7 min. Drain off the juices and reserve.
2 Chop the fennel finely.
3 Melt the butter, add the flour and seasonings. Make the reserved juices up to 275ml ($\frac{1}{2}$pt) with milk and add gradually to the roux, stirring continuously. Stir in the fennel. (If preferred, the sauce may be puréed in a blender at this stage).
4 Heat the sauce for 4–5 min until thickened and bubbling, stirring every 30 secs.
5 Allow the sauce to cool slightly and stir in the cream. Serve hot with fish.

Béchamel sauce *makes about 275ml ($\frac{1}{2}$pt)*
POWER LEVEL: 100% (FULL) OR 50% (DEFROST)

This is basic white sauce but with an excellent flavour.

1 small onion
6 cloves
1 bay leaf
6 peppercorns
1 blade mace
275ml ($\frac{1}{2}$pt) milk
25g (1oz) butter
25g (1oz) flour
salt and pepper

1 Peel the onion and stick with the cloves. Place in a bowl with the rest of the spices and milk.
2 Heat on 100% (full) setting without boiling. Cook on 100% (full) setting for 3 min, stand for 3 min, heat for 2 min, stand for 3 min. Alternatively heat at 50% (defrost) setting for 10–11 min. This allows the infusion of the flavours from the spices into the milk.
3 Melt the butter for 1 min and stir in the flour and the seasonings. Strain the milk and add a little at a time to the butter and flour mixture (called the roux), stirring continuously.
4 Cook on 100% (full) setting for 1$\frac{1}{2}$–2 min, stirring every $\frac{1}{2}$ min until thickened and bubbling. Adjust seasoning if necessary.

Bread sauce *makes about 425ml ($\frac{3}{4}$pt)*
POWER LEVEL: 100% (FULL)
colour page 57

1 medium-sized onion
2 cloves
425ml ($\frac{3}{4}$pt) milk
pinch salt
6 peppercorns
1 bay leaf
25g (1oz) butter
75g (3oz) breadcrumbs

1 Peel the onion but leave it whole. Place in a bowl with the cloves, milk and salt. Heat for 3 min.
2 Add the other ingredients and cook for 5 min, stirring once during cooking.
3 Remove the onion, cloves, peppercorns and bay leaf, then beat well. Beat in an extra 15g ($\frac{1}{2}$oz) butter if required.

Meat or poultry gravy
POWER LEVEL: 100% (FULL)

While the joint is in its final standing period, pour off the meat juices into a jug or gravy boat. Add the usual flavourings or thickening and stock. Heat until cooked, stirring every minute.

Quick white sauce *makes about 275ml (½pt)*
POWER LEVEL: 100% (FULL)

When in a hurry, try this one-stage sauce; although it needs attention whilst cooking, it makes a good quick substitute for the béchamel sauce.

25g (1oz) butter or margarine cut into pieces
25g (1oz) flour
pinch garlic powder
pinch dry mustard
salt and freshly ground black pepper
275ml (½pt) milk

1 Place all the ingredients into a bowl or serving jug and stir briskly or whisk. The ingredients will not combine at this stage.
2 Heat for 3–4 min, stirring or whisking every 15 sec, until cooked and thickened. As the butter or margarine melts it will absorb the flour and, providing the mixture is stirred or whisked frequently, a smooth sauce will be obtained. Adjust seasoning if necessary.

Rum or brandy butter *makes about 225g (½lb)*

Also called hard sauce, this is traditionally served with Christmas pudding, but could also be served with any special hot dessert.

100g (4oz) unsalted butter
100g (4oz) caster sugar
2–3 × 15ml tbsp (2–3 tbsp) rum or brandy

1 Cream the butter, add the sugar gradually, beating well together until the mixture is soft and fluffy.
2 Add the rum or brandy a little at a time, beating well after each addition.
3 Place in the serving bowl and chill in the refrigerator until hard. To make the sauce more decorative, it can be piped into the serving bowl in swirls before chilling.

Cranberry sauce *makes about 275ml (½pt)*
POWER LEVEL: 100% (FULL)
colour page 57

450g (1lb) cranberries, washed
100g (4oz) sugar
1 × 15ml tbsp (1 tbsp) water
25g (1oz) butter

1 Place the cranberries in a covered dish, roasting bag or boiling bag with the sugar and water.
2 Cook for 5–6 min or until the fruit is soft.
3 Add the butter, stir until melted, then cook uncovered for 1 min.
4 Serve hot or cold with roast turkey or chicken.

Bolognaise sauce *(serves 4)*
POWER LEVEL: 100% (FULL) AND 50% (DEFROST)

2 × 15ml tbsp (2 tbsp) oil
1 onion, chopped
2 cloves garlic, finely chopped
2 sticks celery, finely chopped
1 carrot, diced
4 rashers streaky bacon, diced
450g (1lb) minced beef
½ green pepper, diced
4 tomatoes, skinned and chopped
275ml (½pt) boiling stock
2 × 15ml tbsp (2 tbsp) tomato purée
1 bay leaf
1 × 5ml tsp (1 tsp) mixed herbs
pinch nutmeg
salt and pepper
For serving:
freshly cooked spaghetti (page 81)
grated parmesan cheese

1 Heat the oil in a large bowl for 2 min on 100% (full) setting. Add the onion, garlic, celery and carrot, cover and cook on 100% (full) setting for 3 min.
2 Add the bacon and cook on 100% (full) setting for 2 min, then add the minced beef, stir well and cook for a further 2 min.
3 Stir in all the remaining ingredients and season well. Cook on 100% (full) setting for 10 min and stir, reduce to 50% (defrost) setting, cook for 20 min. Adjust seasoning to taste. Serve with freshly cooked spaghetti and grated parmesan cheese.

Tomato sauce *makes about 275ml (½pt)*
POWER LEVEL: 100% (FULL)

1 × 15ml tbsp (1 tbsp) olive oil
1 large onion, peeled and finely chopped
1–2 cloves garlic, crushed or finely chopped
400g (14oz) can tomatoes, drained
1 × 15ml tbsp (1 tbsp) tomato purée
1 glass red wine or juice from tomatoes
few sprigs fresh herbs, or
1 × 5ml tsp (1 tsp) dried herbs, eg thyme or rosemary
salt and freshly ground black pepper

1 Place olive oil, onion and garlic into a bowl and toss well. Cook for 4–5 min until soft.
2 Roughly chop the tomatoes and add to the bowl with the remaining ingredients.
3 Cook uncovered until soft and the liquid quantity is reduced giving a fairly thick sauce, stirring every 3 min.
4 Use when referred to in recipes or where a good, well-flavoured tomato sauce is required, ie as a topping for pizzas or to mix with plain boiled pasta.

Cornflour sauce *makes about 275ml ($\frac{1}{2}$pt)*
POWER LEVEL: 100% (FULL)

1 × 15ml tbsp (1 tbsp) sugar
1 × 15ml tbsp (1 tbsp) cornflour
275ml ($\frac{1}{2}$pt) milk
few drops vanilla essence

1 Mix the sugar and cornflour together with a little of the milk. Gradually add the rest of the milk and the vanilla essence.
2 Cook for 3–4 min until thick, stirring every minute.

Custard sauce
colour page 57
Follow the ingredients and method for cornflour sauce substituting custard powder for the cornflour.

Egg custard sauce *makes about 275ml ($\frac{1}{2}$pt)*
POWER LEVEL: 100% (FULL) or 50% (DEFROST)

2 egg yolks
25g (1oz) caster sugar
15g ($\frac{1}{2}$oz) cornflour
275ml ($\frac{1}{2}$pt) milk
few drops vanilla essence

1 Place the egg yolks in a bowl with the sugar and mix well.
2 Blend the cornflour smoothly with the milk and heat in the microwave for 2–3 min on 100% (full) setting, stirring every minute.
3 Pour the milk onto the egg and sugar mixture and stir well. Add the vanilla essence and stir again. Cook on 100% (full) setting for 2 min, stirring every 30 sec.

Note: *For models with a defrost control the custard can be cooked for 4–4$\frac{1}{2}$ min on 50% (defrost) to avoid overcooking.*

Hollandaise sauce *(serves 4)*
POWER LEVEL: 50% (DEFROST)
colour page 36

Serve with freshly cooked asparagus, broccoli or globe artichokes as a starter to a meal.

100g (4oz) butter
2 × 15ml tbsp (2 tbsp) wine vinegar
2 egg yolks
salt and pepper

1 Melt the butter on 50% (defrost) setting for 2 min, add the vinegar and egg yolks and whisk lightly.
2 Cook on 50% (defrost) setting for 1 min, whisk well, season and serve immediately.

DO NOT FREEZE

Barbecue sauce *makes about 275ml ($\frac{1}{2}$pt)*
POWER LEVEL: 100% (FULL)

15g ($\frac{1}{2}$oz) butter
1 onion, finely chopped
2 × 5ml tsp (2 tsp) worcestershire sauce
6 × 15ml tbsp (6 tbsp) tomato ketchup
225ml (8fl oz) water
salt and pepper

1 Melt the butter in the microwave for 1 min. Add the onion, cover and cook for 3 min.
2 Add the remaining ingredients, stir well and cook for a further 3 min.

Note: *Serve the sauce with beefburgers, chicken or any barbecued food.*

Curry sauce *makes about 550ml (1pt)*
POWER LEVEL: 100% (FULL) AND 30%

150ml ($\frac{1}{4}$pt) milk
25g (1oz) desiccated coconut
50g (2oz) butter
1 onion, chopped
1 apple, peeled and diced
1–2 × 15ml tbsp (1–2 tbsp) curry powder
2 × 15ml tbsp (2 tbsp) plain flour
550ml (1pt) boiling stock
2 × 15ml tbsp (2 tbsp) chutney
25g (1oz) sultanas
salt and pepper
pinch cayenne pepper

1 Heat the milk and coconut together in a small dish for 1$\frac{1}{2}$ min on 100% (full) setting. Stir, leave for 10 min to infuse the flavours.
2 Melt the butter in a medium-sized bowl for 1$\frac{1}{2}$–2 min on 100% (full) setting. Add the onion and apple and cook on 100% (full) setting for 3 min.
3 Stir in curry powder and flour, mixing thoroughly. Cook for a further 1 min.
4 Add the boiling stock gradually, beating well after each addition.
5 Strain the coconut milk into the sauce through a sieve. Add the remaining ingredients.
6 Bring to the boil on 100% (full) setting, stirring every 2 min.
7 Cover and cook on 30% setting for 10–15 min to allow flavours to blend, stirring occasionally.

Thatched Tuna Pie (page 50) and Cottage Pie (page 67)

Fish

All fish cooked by microwave is simply out of this world – full of flavour and cooked to perfection – whether it is frozen, fresh, canned or boil-in-the-bag fish. If steaming, baking or poaching fresh fish either whole or filleted, it should be cleaned and prepared in the normal way and covered during cooking. Normally a little melted butter and/or lemon juice is sufficient additional moisture. Sprinkle with a little seasoning, paprika or herbs to enhance the appearance and flavour. The tail ends of thin fillets or fish may be overlapped or covered with aluminium foil to prevent overcooking of these thinner parts. Test the fish at regular intervals – when cooked the flesh will flake.

Although most fish is cooked using a 100% (full) setting, when reheating fish in a sauce use a lower setting to ensure the dish is evenly heated throughout. Boil-in-the-bag fish should have the plastic bag pierced before cooking in the microwave. Breadcrumbed fish may be dotted or brushed with a little butter, although the breadcrumbed coating will not become crisp unless you use a browning dish (page 10). Do not attempt to deep fat fry in the microwave as the temperature of the fat cannot be controlled.

Fish defrosting and cooking chart

Fish	Defrost time 50% (defrost)	Cooking time 100% (full)
White fish, eg cod, haddock, coley fillets or cutlets, plaice or sole, 450g (1lb) prepared fillets	5 min Stand for 5 min	4–5 min
Smoked fish, eg smoked haddock, cod, 450g (1lb) prepared fillets	5 min Stand for 5 min	4–5 min
Mackerel 2 × 275–350g (10–12oz) fish, gutted but whole	5 min Stand for 5 min 2–3 min Stand for 3 min	8–10 min
1 kipper	—	1–2 min
Herrings and trout 2 × 225g (8oz) fish, gutted but whole	4 min Stand for 4 min 4 min Stand for 5 min	6–8 min
Salmon steaks, 450g (1lb)	5 min Stand for 5 min	4–5 min
Shell fish, eg scampi, prawns, 450g (1lb) prepared	4 min Stand for 5 min	Use as recipe directs
Fish in sauce, 200g (7oz) bag	3 min Stand for 5 min	3–4 min
Boil-in-the-bag fillets 200g (7oz)	3 min Stand for 5 min	3 min
Kipper fillets 225g (8oz)	3 min Stand for 5 min	3 min

Thatched tuna pie (serves 4–6)
POWER LEVEL: 100% (FULL)
colour page 49

25g (1oz) butter or margarine
2 medium leeks, trimmed and finely sliced
275ml ($\frac{1}{2}$pt) béchamel sauce (page 46)
4 tomatoes, skinned and quartered
450g (1lb) canned tuna fish, approximately
1 × 15ml tbsp (1 tbsp) chopped parsley
$\frac{1}{2}$ lemon, grated rind and juice
salt and freshly ground black pepper
50g (2oz) fresh brown breadcrumbs
50g (2oz) red leicester cheese, finely grated
grated nutmeg for sprinkling
For garnish:
parsley sprigs

1 Melt the butter or margarine in a large, round, shallow dish for 1 min, toss in the leeks, cover and cook for 3–4 min. Add the sauce and the tomatoes.
2 Drain and flake the tuna and add to the sauce with the parsley, lemon rind and juice and seasoning.

Mix well together, smooth the top and clean the edges of the dish.
3 Mix the breadcrumbs with the grated cheese and sprinkle over the top of the sauce mixture. Sprinkle with a little grated nutmeg.
4 Cook for 6 min, turning every 2 min, until heated through.
5 Serve hot garnished with parsley sprigs.

Roll mops (serves 4)
POWER LEVEL: 100% (FULL)

4 fresh herrings
1 blade mace
1 bay leaf
2 cloves
6 peppercorns
pinch salt
1 onion, chopped
150ml ($\frac{1}{4}$pt) water
150ml ($\frac{1}{4}$pt) vinegar

1 Clean and bone the herrings. Roll up tightly from the tail end. Secure with a wooden cocktail stick if necessary.
2 Place in a shallow dish with the herbs, seasoning and onion. Mix the water and vinegar together and pour over the fish. Cover the dish with a lid or clingfilm.
3 Cook in the microwave for 6–7 min. Allow to cool in the cooking liquor.
4 Serve cold as a starter or with salad.

Tomato fish charlotte (*serves 4*)
POWER LEVEL: 100% (FULL)

450g (1lb) cod or haddock fillet
25g (1oz) butter
½ lemon, juice and grated rind
100g (4oz) white breadcrumbs
5–6 × 15ml tbsp (5–6 tbsp) oil
275ml (½pt) tomato sauce (page 47)
For garnish:
tomato slices

1 Lightly grease a large round dish or pie dish.
2 Skin the cod or haddock fillet, place in the greased dish, dot with the butter. Sprinkle with the lemon juice, cover and cook for 4–5 min, turning once. Drain the liquid from the fish.
3 Preheat a browning dish for 5–6 min.
4 Sprinkle the breadcrumbs with the oil, mix well to ensure they are coated with the oil.
5 Add the breadcrumbs to the preheated browning dish and cook uncovered for 1–2 min until lightly browned, stirring every ½ min. Stir in the grated lemon rind.
6 Heat the tomato sauce for 2–3 min and pour on top of the fish. Smooth the top and sprinkle on the breadcrumbs. Cook for 2–3 min until hot through.
7 Serve hot garnished with tomato slices.

Fish pie
POWER LEVEL: 100% (FULL)

1 × 298g (10½oz) can condensed vegetable soup
150ml (¼pt) milk
3 × 15ml tbsp (3 tbsp) frozen peas
450g (1lb) cooked fish
salt and pepper
75g (3oz) crisps
50g (2oz) cheddar cheese, grated
For garnish:
1 × 15ml tbsp (1 tbsp) chopped parsley

1 Put the soup and milk into an ovenware dish. Heat for 1 min, stir, heat for 2 min. Mix thoroughly.
2 Add the peas and cooked fish and pour into a 850ml (1½pt) pie dish. Cook for 4 min, stirring once during cooking.

3 Sprinkle half the crisps on top of the mixture, cover with the cheese and top with the remaining crisps.
4 Cook for 1½ min, or until the cheese is melted. Garnish with chopped parsley and serve.

DO NOT FREEZE THE COMPLETE DISH – THE CRISP TOPPING SHOULD BE ADDED AFTER THAWING

Fish pudding (*serves 4–5*)
POWER LEVEL: 100% (FULL)

This pudding is very light in texture and makes a good lunch or supper dish.

450g (1lb) white fish fillets, cooked
75g (3oz) white breadcrumbs
1 × 15ml tbsp (1 tbsp) chopped parsley
1 lemon, grated rind
salt and freshly ground black pepper
50g (2oz) butter or margarine
2 eggs, beaten
For serving:
tomato sauce (page 47)

1 Lightly grease a 850ml (1½pt) pudding basin.
2 Flake the fish, discarding any skin or bones. Mix with the breadcrumbs, parsley, lemon rind and seasoning.
3 Melt the butter for 1–1½ min and add to the fish with the beaten eggs. Mix well together.
4 Place in the greased pudding basin. Cover with clingfilm making a slit with the pointed end of a sharp knife.
5 Cook for 4–5 min, turning once halfway through.
6 Remove clingfilm and invert onto the serving dish.
7 Serve hot with tomato sauce or cold with a dressed salad.

Trout and almonds (*serves 4*)
POWER LEVEL: 100% (FULL)

4 trout (about 100–150g (4–5oz) each)
salt and pepper
few drops lemon juice
50g (2oz) butter
50–75g (2–3oz) flaked almonds, toasted
For serving:
lemon wedges

1 Clean the fish, leaving the heads on. Wash and dry. Place in the serving dish, season lightly and add a few drops of lemon juice.
2 Melt the butter, in the microwave, for 2 min. Brush the trout with the butter, cover with kitchen paper and cook for 6 min.
3 Sprinkle almonds over the fish and cook for a further 2–4 min, depending on the size of the fish. Larger fish will take 1–2 min longer.
4 Serve hot with lemon wedges.

Scampi provençale (*serves 4*)
POWER LEVEL: 100% (FULL)
colour photograph opposite

25g (1oz) butter
1 onion, chopped
1 clove garlic, chopped
1 × 397g (14oz) can tomatoes, drained
5 × 15ml tbsp (5 tbsp) dry white wine
salt and pepper
pinch sugar
1 × 15ml tbsp (1 tbsp) chopped parsley
225g (8oz) scampi
For serving:
boiled rice (page 81)

1 Melt the butter in a casserole dish for 1 min. Toss the onion and garlic in the butter and cook for 4 min.
2 Add tomatoes, wine, seasoning, sugar and parsley. Stir well and heat for 3 min.
3 Drain the scampi well, add to the sauce and cook for about 2 min or until just heated through. Serve with freshly boiled rice.

Skate with caper butter (*serves 4*)
POWER LEVEL: 100% (FULL)
colour photograph opposite

2 wings of skate (about 450g (1lb) each)
50–75g (2–3oz) butter
1 × 15ml tbsp (1 tbsp) capers
5 × 15ml tbsp (5 tbsp) wine vinegar
1 × 15ml tbsp (1 tbsp) chopped parsley
salt and pepper

1 Cut each wing into 3 wedges. Place in a large, shallow dish covered in clingfilm and cook for 5 min.
2 Melt and cook the butter for 5 min. Add the capers, vinegar, parsley and seasoning and cook for 2 min.
3 Skin the skate and lay the pieces in the serving dish. Pour the caper butter over the fish, cover and reheat for 3–4 min.
4 Serve hot.

Smoked fish flan (*serves 6*)
POWER LEVEL: 100% (FULL) AND 50% (DEFROST)

175g (6oz) rich shortcrust pastry (page 32)
1 medium leek, washed and finely sliced
salt and pepper
225g (8oz) smoked cod or haddock, cooked
2 hardboiled eggs, sliced
275ml (½pt) béchamel sauce (page 46)
50g (2oz) cheese, finely grated
450g (1lb) creamed potatoes (page 76)
For garnish:
parsley sprigs

1 Roll out the pastry, line a 20cm (8in) flan dish and bake blind (page 32).
2 Place the leek in a boiling or roasting bag or covered casserole dish with a sprinkling of salt and 2–3 × 15ml tbsp (2–3 tbsp) water and cook on 100% (full) setting for 4–5 min. Drain off the water.
3 Flake the fish discarding any bones or skin and place in the bottom of the flan case with the leek.
4 Arrange the slices of hardboiled egg on the top, sprinkle with salt and pepper and cover with the béchamel sauce.
5 Beat half the cheese into the potato and place the mixture in a forcing bag with a large star nozzle. Pipe the potato around the edge and across the middle of the flan.
6 Heat through on 50% (defrost) setting for 9–10 min, turning every 3–4 min.
7 Sprinkle with the remaining cheese and cook on 100% (full) setting for 1 min until the cheese is melted. Alternatively brown under a hot grill.
8 Serve garnished with parsley.

DO NOT FREEZE

Salmon with white wine sauce (*serves 2*)
POWER LEVEL: 50% (DEFROST)

2 × 200–225g (7–8oz) salmon cutlets
salt and pepper
150ml (¼pt) white wine sauce (page 46)
1 egg yolk
3 × 15ml tbsp (3 tbsp) single cream
For garnish:
shrimps or prawns
parsley and lemon butterflies

1 Wash the cutlets, place in a dish and sprinkle with salt and pepper. Cover with clingfilm and cook for 10–12 min, turning once.
2 Make up the white wine sauce as directed using the salmon juices. Cool the sauce slightly.
3 While the sauce is cooling, reheat the salmon steaks in a serving dish for 2 min.
4 Stir the egg yolk and cream into the sauce. Check and adjust the seasoning.
5 Pour the sauce over the salmon. Sprinkle with a few prepared shrimps or prawns and garnish with parsley and lemon butterflies.

FREEZE THE SAUCE SEPARATELY

Crab gratinée diable (*serves 2–4*)
POWER LEVEL: 100% (FULL)

25g (1oz) butter
1 dressed crab, or 350g (12oz) canned or frozen crabmeat
25g (1oz) cheese, grated

2 × 15ml tbsp (2 tbsp) fresh white breadcrumbs
1 × 15ml tbsp (1 tbsp) single cream or top of the milk
pinch each dry mustard and cayenne pepper
dash anchovy essence
1 firm banana
few drops lemon juice
For garnish:
1 × 15ml tbsp (1 tbsp) chopped parsley
For serving:
dry biscuits or fingers of toast

1 Melt the butter, in a bowl, for 1 min. Add the prepared crab meat, cheese, breadcrumbs, cream and seasonings.
2 Mix thoroughly and carefully spoon back into the cleaned crab shell, or into a small bowl.
3 Cook for 2 min, stand for 5 min, turn, cook for 2 min.
4 Slice the banana thinly and dip in the lemon juice to prevent the slices from browning. Place around the outside of the shell or dish and cook for 1 min.
5 Sprinkle with chopped parsley and serve with dry biscuits or fingers of toast.

DO NOT FREEZE

Salmon-stuffed pancakes
POWER LEVEL: 100% (FULL)

1 × 198g (7oz) can salmon, drained and flaked
1 × 5ml tsp (1 tsp) mustard
1 × 15ml tbsp (1 tbsp) onion, finely chopped
275ml ($\frac{1}{2}$pt) white sauce (page 46)
salt and pepper
8 × 20cm (8in) cooked pancakes (page 54)
2 × 15ml tbsp (2 tbsp) lemon juice
150ml ($\frac{1}{4}$pt) soured cream
For garnish:
2 × 15ml tbsp (2 tbsp) chopped chives

1 Stir the salmon, mustard and onion into the white sauce. Season to taste.
2 Spread an equal amount of sauce on each pancake and roll up. Lay the pancakes in a shallow serving dish and moisten with the lemon juice.
3 Cover the dish with clingfilm and cook in the microwave for 8 min, giving $\frac{1}{4}$ turn every 2 min.
4 Top with soured cream and garnish with the chopped chives. Serve immediately.

Skate with Caper Butter (page 52) and Scampi Provençale (page 52)

Pancakes

Pancakes cannot be successfully cooked in the microwave, so are best cooked conventionally; this basic pancake batter is sufficient to make 8–10 thin pancakes.

100g (4oz) plain flour
pinch salt
1 egg, beaten
275ml ($\frac{1}{2}$pt) milk
oil for frying

1 Sift the flour and salt into a mixing bowl. Make a well in the centre and drop in the beaten egg.
2 Slowly pour on half the milk, mixing the egg and milk into the flour with a wooden spoon.
3 Beat the mixture with a wooden spoon or whisk until smooth and free of lumps.
4 Add the remaining milk, whisking continually until the mixture is bubbly and the consistency of single cream.
5 Heat a 17.5cm (7–8in) frying pan on a conventional hotplate or burner. Just sufficient oil should be added to prevent the pancakes from sticking.
6 The pan and oil should be really hot. Pour in just enough batter to allow a thin film to coat the base of the pan, tilting the pan to spread the mixture.
7 The base of the pancake should be cooked in about 1 min. Flip the pancake over with a palette knife or spatula and cook the other side for about 1 min. If the pancakes are taking too long to cook, adjust the heat or make sure that too much batter is not being used.
8 Layer the pancakes in absorbent kitchen paper and keep warm if to be used immediately. Alternatively, leave to cool, or freeze as they may be thawed and reheated most satisfactorily in the microwave.
9 Fill and use as required, allowing one per person if served as a starter to a meal or two if served as a snack or as a main course with vegetables.

Note: *The ingredients for the pancake batter may be blended in a liquidiser or food processor.*

Seafood flan *(serves 6)*
POWER LEVEL: 100% (FULL)
colour page 15

175g (6oz) rich shortcrust pastry (page 32)
150ml ($\frac{1}{4}$pt) béchamel sauce (page 46)
salt and pepper
225g (8oz) crabmeat, fresh or frozen
150ml ($\frac{1}{4}$pt) mayonnaise
few drops lemon juice
2 hardboiled eggs, chopped
150ml ($\frac{1}{4}$pt) double cream, whipped
For garnish:
thinly sliced cucumber and chopped parsley

1 Roll out the pastry, line a 20cm (8in) flan dish and bake blind (page 32). Leave to cool.
2 Beat the béchamel sauce and add seasoning. Mix in the crabmeat, mayonnaise, lemon juice and chopped hardboiled egg. Finally fold in the whipped double cream.
3 Pour the mixture into the cooled flan case and smooth the top. Chill until set.
4 Serve cold garnished with cucumber slices and chopped parsley as a starter to a meal or as a main course with mixed salad.

DO NOT FREEZE

Variations
Cooked and shelled prawns, scampi, mussels, scallops, lobster, fresh or canned tuna or salmon or a mixture of these can be used as alternatives to the crabmeat.

Scallop and mushroom pie *(serves 6–8)*
POWER LEVEL: 100% (FULL)

This makes an excellent fish course or main course for a dinner party.

16 scallops, cleaned
275ml ($\frac{1}{2}$pt) milk
salt and freshly ground black pepper
50g (2oz) butter
25g (1oz) flour
175g (6oz) mushrooms, washed and sliced
150ml ($\frac{1}{4}$pt) dry white wine
450g (1lb) creamed potatoes (page 76)
For garnish:
parsley sprigs

1 Lightly grease a large shallow round ovenware dish.
2 Cut each scallop into 4, place with the milk and seasonings into a bowl and cook for 3–4 min. Drain and reserve the milk.
3 Melt 25g (1oz) butter for 1 min, stir in the flour until smooth. Gradually stir in the reserved milk.
4 Cook for 3–4 min until thick, stirring every minute. Beat well until smooth. Mix in scallops, mushrooms and wine.
5 Cover with piped creamed potatoes and top with slivers of the remaining butter.
6 Cook for 6–8 min or until hot through, turning every 2 min.
7 Garnish with parsley and serve hot with a side salad.

Variation
King-size prawns may replace the scallops. Peel the prawns and add to the sauce, made from the butter, flour and milk, with the mushrooms and wine. Continue as above.

Sole véronique (*serves 4*)
POWER LEVEL: 100% (FULL)

2 soles, filleted
3 slices onion
50g (2oz) button mushrooms, sliced
few sprigs parsley
1 bay leaf
salt and pepper
150ml ($\frac{1}{4}$pt) dry white wine
150ml ($\frac{1}{4}$pt) water
100g (4oz) white grapes
25g (1oz) butter
25g (1oz) plain flour
150ml ($\frac{1}{4}$pt) milk, approximately
squeeze lemon juice
2 × 15ml tbsp (2 tbsp) single cream

1 Trim the fillets, wash, wipe and lay them in a large shallow dish. Add the onion, mushrooms, herbs, seasoning, wine and water. Cover and cook for 5 min. Drain and reserve the stock.
2 Place the grapes in hot water for a few minutes, then peel, halve and remove pips, reserving a few halves for decoration.
3 Melt the butter in a large bowl for 1 min, stir in the flour and the fish stock, made up to 275ml ($\frac{1}{2}$pt) with the milk. Cook in the microwave for 3–4 min, stirring every minute.
4 Stir in the grapes, lemon juice and cream and pour the sauce over the fish. Reheat in the microwave for 3 min, then decorate with the reserved grapes and serve.

Cod steaks with leek and corn stuffing
(*serves 4*)
POWER LEVEL: 100% (FULL)

1 leek, washed and trimmed
40g (1$\frac{1}{2}$oz) butter
50g (2oz) white breadcrumbs
40g (1$\frac{1}{2}$oz) cheddar cheese, grated
1 × 326g (11$\frac{1}{2}$oz) can sweetcorn
salt and pepper
2 tomatoes, skinned
1 egg, beaten
4 cod steaks, weighing about 175g (6oz) each

1 Slice the leek and place in a bowl with 2 × 15ml tbsp (2 tbsp) salted water. Cover with clingfilm and cook for 3 min.
2 Melt the butter in the microwave for 1–1$\frac{1}{2}$ min. Add to the leek with the breadcrumbs, cheese, sweetcorn and seasoning, reserving 2 × 15ml tbsp (2 tbsp) of sweetcorn for garnish.
3 Chop one of the tomatoes and add it to the mixture. Bind the stuffing with the beaten egg.
4 Wash and trim the fish. Place in a large casserole and season lightly. Cover and cook for 5 min, then stand for 5 min.
5 Fill the cavity and cover the end of each steak with the stuffing.
6 Slice the remaining tomato and place one slice on each steak. Sprinkle on the reserved corn.
7 Cover and cook for 3 min, turn and cook for 3 min. Serve immediately.

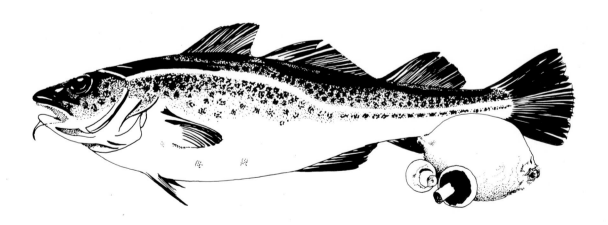

Meat and poultry

Large and small cuts of meat and poultry can be successfully cooked by microwave and the advantage when roasting a joint is that while the meat is resting during its final standing period, vegetables, sauces and gravies can be quickly prepared to produce a complete microwave meal.

The microwave cooker will not tenderise meat in the same way as the conventional cooker, so prime cuts give the better results. Cheaper cuts should be tenderised or marinaded in oil and vinegar for several hours before cooking, or alternatively chop into small pieces or put through a mincer.

The advantage of cooking meat casseroles by microwave is that they can be prepared well in advance, then refrigerated or frozen and just reheated when required. Casseroles are more tender if, after cooking, they are left to cool naturally and then reheated before serving.

Defrosting

Although thinner cuts of meat can be thawed and cooked in one heating operation, generally it is better to ensure that all meat and poultry is completely defrosted before cooking to ensure even results. This can be carried out by using the microwave, or by thawing naturally or a combination of both, commencing the defrosting in the microwave and then leaving the meat to thaw thoroughly in the refrigerator, larder or at room temperature.

When defrosting by microwave, thinner ends of joints and smaller cuts can be protected with smooth pieces of aluminium foil which prevent the outer sections from beginning to cook while the centre parts are still thawing. If some cooking does begin during defrosting, this is acceptable providing the meat is to be cooked immediately afterwards, although the partially cooked parts should be protected with aluminium foil during the cooking process.

To ensure even defrosting, the food should be turned halfway through the defrosting process; smaller cuts – such as chops, steak, chicken portions and sausages – should be separated and turned as soon as possible after defrosting begins. When defrosting sausage meat or minced meat, the thawed portions can be removed leaving the still-frozen part to be returned to the microwave.

Most meats require standing time to allow heat equalisation during defrosting so that the outer parts will not begin to cook while the centre is still frozen, but foods covered with clingfilm or placed in a roasting bag will retain more moisture and defrosting will be slightly faster.

Meat thermometers must not be used in the microwave during a defrosting or heating cycle. Only specially designed thermometers may be left inside the oven while it is operating. The use of a thermometer is helpful to determine the temperature at the centre of the food, particularly when thawing larger cuts and joints.

Cooking

A joint will have a better appearance and cook more evenly if it is a regular shape. Ideal cuts are top leg of pork, lamb and rolled joints. If the meat is not uniform in size, the narrower sections may by covered with a smooth piece of aluminium foil for half the cooking time. Poultry should have the wings and legs tied closely to the body and any projecting parts should be protected by covering them with foil.

Seasonings may be sprinkled over the meat but salt attracts moisture and may cause a hardening effect on the outer edges during cooking. If in doubt, leave any seasoning until after cooking. The exception to this rule is the skin on pork which should be scored with a knife and rubbed with salt to help obtain a crisp crackling.

Roasting bags are ideal for cooking all joints in the microwave, but do remember not to use the paper/metal ties; string or rubber bands are suitable and may be used instead. Alternatively, meat may be cooked in a covered casserole dish or can be 'open' roasted. This latter method is preferable when cooking pork with crackling as it allows a certain amount of moisture to 'escape'. When 'open' roasting the joint is placed on an inverted small flat dish or

Roast Turkey (page 59), Bread Sauce (page 46), Cranberry Sauce (page 47), Christmas Pudding (page 88) and Custard Sauce (page 48)

Lamb Portugaise (page 63) and Rice Pudding (page 89)

plate which is used as a trivet inside the roasting dish. Specially designed microwave roasting dishes and trivets are now available on the market. These keep the joint out of its own juices during cooking, but the meat should be lightly covered with greaseproof paper or kitchen paper to prevent splatterings on to the oven interior. It is preferable to turn larger joints at least once during their cooking period and they should be allowed to stand for 10–25 minutes halfway through. Joints which have fat on one side only should be placed with the fat side down at the commencement of cooking and turned fat side up halfway through the cooking period.

If the total cooking time is 15 minutes or more the joint will brown naturally but for extra browning the joint may be placed in a conventional oven at a high temperature for 10–15 minutes at the end of the microwave cooking period, or placed under a hot grill. The careful use of gravy brownings, sauces or paprika pepper, painted or sprinkled on to the surface of the joint, will give a more attractive colour if required. Steaks, chops, sausages and chicken joints etc may be browned during cooking by using a browning dish (page 10) or alternatively finished off under a hot grill after cooking by microwave.

At the end of the microwave cooking period allow the joint to stand for at least 5 minutes and up to 20 minutes to heat equalise. The joint will carry on cooking slightly during this period, but do leave it in the roasting bag or cover it with aluminium foil to retain the heat. However, if the joint is cooked to the desired degree on completion of the microwave cooking period, it is not necessary to let it stand.

Casseroles and stews may be prepared and cooked in the microwave cooker using 100% (full) setting for half the cooking time, then reducing to a lower setting, ie 50% (defrost), for the remaining time; or cook on this lower setting for the entire cooking time. This will allow food flavourings and seasonings to blend during this slower cooking stage. The casserole may be frozen whole or in individual portions – whichever is the most convenient. During defrosting and reheating, allow approximately 1 minute per 25g (1oz) using a 100% (full) setting, or use a lower setting for a longer period.

The defrosting and cooking charts given here are based on meats which have been removed straight from the freezer for defrosting and are fully thawed before cooking. If meats are partially thawed before being placed in the microwave for defrosting or are not completely thawed before cooking then the times on these charts will require some adjustment to suit. The defrosting standing times given is the total resting time required and a better result is obtained if this time is spread evenly throughout the defrosting period, allowing short bursts of microwave energy interspersed with standing times.

Longer periods of microwave energy exposure with standing times will obtain a quicker defrost but may result in a less even thawing. For those microwave models with a defrost control or setting do not forget to read the section on page 15.

The cooking times given are when using a 100% (full) setting. For those microwave cookers with a 'roast' setting, it is advisable to check with the manufacturer's recommendations for timings when using a lower setting. Some joints benefit from a slow cook using a 50% (defrost) setting in which case the cooking time will be almost double. Alternatively, the joint may be cooked for half the time on 100% (full) setting and then reduced to 50% (defrost) for the remaining time. Much depends on the time available and your own preferences.

Points to remember

1 The tenderness of meat casseroles is improved if the dish is left to cool after microwave cooking and then reheated when required.
2 A joint will have a better appearance and cook more evenly if it is a regular shape.
3 Smooth pieces of aluminium foil may be used to protect the thinner or narrower ends of meat during defrosting and/or cooking.
4 Meat and poultry should be fully thawed before cooking.
5 Joints should be turned halfway through the cooking cycle.
6 Standing time is required by most joints at the end of the cooking time but larger joints require a standing time halfway through their cooking period.
7 Standing time is also required during the defrost period for most joints to allow the heat to equalise throughout the food. This ensures even thawing of the meat.
8 The defrosting and cooking times on the following chart include timings for lower and higher output cookers; the models with lower output will require the longer times and those with a higher output will require the shorter times, ie beef medium 5–7 min per $\frac{1}{2}$kg (1lb).
9 Allow an extra minute per $\frac{1}{2}$kg (1lb) when cooking stuffed poultry or joints.

Defrosting and cooking joints

Meat	Defrost time 50% (defrost)	Cooking time 100% (full)	Special points
	½kg (1lb)	½kg (1lb)	
Beef Rolled, boned	8–10 min Stand for 50–60 min	Rare = 4–6 min Med = 5–7 min Well = 6–8 min Stand for 15–25 min	Turn joint on sides during defrosting.
Beef Joints on bone	12 min Stand for 60–70 min	Rare = 4–6 min Med = 5–7 min Well = 6–8 min Stand for 15–25 min	Cover bone end with foil during defrosting.
Lamb or veal Leg	6 min Stand for 30–40 min	7–9 min Stand for 15–30 min	Cover knuckle end of lamb with foil once thawed.
Lamb or veal Shoulder	5 min Stand for 20–30 min	7–9 min Stand for 15–30 min	Foreleg and rib (if any) may need covering with foil during defrosting.
Pork Top leg of pork	7–8 min Stand for 60–70 min	7–9 min Stand for 15–30 min	Try to get an evenly shaped joint. Tie for roasting after thawing.
POULTRY Chicken Whole unboned	6–7 min Stand for 20–30 min	5–7 min Stand for 5–10 min	Drumsticks may need to be covered with foil for the first half of the cooking period, to prevent overcooking.
Turkey Whole unboned	5–7 min Stand for 2–3 hr	6–8 min Stand for 35–45 min	Legs and wings need to be covered with foil as for chicken.
Duckling Whole unboned	6–7 min Stand for 30–40 min	5–7 min Stand for 5–10 min	Legs and wings may need to be covered with foil as for chicken.

Defrosting smaller cuts

Type or cut of meat	Defrosting time 50% (defrost)	Standing time	Special points	Cooking
Stewing or braising meat, eg beef or lamb 675g (1½lb)	11–12 min	10 min	Separate pieces of meat during defrosting.	Use as required.
Minced beef 450g (1lb)	10–11 min	11 min	Break up during defrosting. Remove thawed meat from oven.	Use as required.
Belly pork strips 450g (1lb) (4 strips)	4–5 min	5 min	Separate strips during defrosting.	Use as required or cook for 8–10 min, turning during cooking.
Offal (liver and kidney) 450g (1lb)	9–10 min	4 min	Separate pieces during defrosting.	Use as required.
Sausagemeat 450g (1lb)	6–7 min	10 min	Break thawed sausagemeat up and remove from oven during defrosting.	Use as required.
Sausages 450g (1lb)	6–7 min	10 min	Separate during defrosting.	Prick skins and cook for 9–10 min

Type or cut of meat	Defrosting time 50% (defrost)	Standing time	Special points	Cooking
Bacon 225g (8oz)	4–5 min	5 min	Separate rashers during defrosting.	5–6 min.
Lamb chops 2 × 100g (4oz)	4–5 min	5 min	Separate chops during defrosting.	5–6 min.
Pork chops 2 × 225g (8oz)	6–8 min	10 min	Separate chops during defrosting.	10–11 min.
Chicken portions 1 × 275–375g (10–13oz)	7–8 min	10 min	If necessary protect with aluminium foil during cooking.	5–7 min.

Steak and kidney suet crust pie (serves 4)

POWER LEVEL: 100% (FULL) AND 50% (DEFROST)

An alternative to the traditional steak and kidney pudding, this dish has suet crust pastry over the top of the meat only.

25g (1oz) butter or margarine
1 medium onion, peeled and chopped
450g (1lb) chuck steak
3 lambs' kidneys
25g (1oz) flour
salt and freshly ground black pepper
425ml (¾pt) beef stock, boiling
100g (4oz) suet crust pastry (page 61)

1 Melt the butter or margarine in a bowl for 1 min on 100% (full) setting, add the onion and toss well in the butter. Cook for a further 2 min.
2 Trim any fat from the meat and cut into 1.25cm (½in) dice. Skin and core the kidneys, cut into small pieces and add to the meat.
3 Mix the flour and seasonings, add to the meat and toss in the flour. Add to the onion and mix well.
4 Cook on 100% (full) setting for 5–6 min until the meat is browned and add the boiling stock. Stir, cover and heat until boiling for approximately 3–4 min.
5 With the microwave on 50% (defrost) setting, continue to cook the meat for a further 25–30 min.
6 Drain off most of the gravy and reserve. Place the meat into a 700–850ml (1¼–1½pt) oval pie dish and smooth the top.
7 Roll out the pastry into an oval to fit the inside of the dish. Cover the meat with the pastry and press into the side edges of the dish.
8 Cover loosely with clingfilm slit with the pointed end of a sharp knife and cook on 100% (full) setting for 4½–5 min, turning once halfway through.
9 Serve hot, serving the reserved gravy separately.

Kidney and bacon casserole (serves 4)

POWER LEVEL: 100% (FULL)

450g (1lb) lambs' kidneys
1 × 15ml tbsp (1 tbsp) plain flour
2 × 5ml tsp (2 tsp) gravy powder
1 × 5ml tsp (1 tsp) mixed herbs
pinch garlic granules
salt and pepper
1 × 15ml tbsp (1 tbsp) oil
1 onion, chopped
4 rashers streaky bacon, diced
1 carrot, thinly sliced
1 × 396g (14oz) can tomatoes
1 stock cube
boiling water
dash worcestershire sauce
100g (4oz) mushrooms, sliced
1 × 15ml tbsp (1 tbsp) cornflour
For garnish:
1 × 15ml tbsp (1 tbsp) chopped parsley
For serving:
suet dumplings (page 61), optional

1 Halve the kidneys and remove any skin and core. Season the flour with gravy powder, herbs, garlic, salt and pepper. Toss the kidneys in the flour.
2 Heat the oil in a large casserole dish for 1 min. Add the onion and bacon and cook for 2 min. Add the kidneys, cover and cook for 2 min.
3 Add the carrot. Drain the tomatoes, reserving the juice. Crumble the stock cube into the tomato juice and make the liquid up to 275ml (½pt) with boiling water.
4 Add the tomatoes, liquid and worcestershire sauce to the casserole. Cook, still covered, for 10 min, stand for 5 min. Add the mushrooms, replace the lid and cook for 5 min.
5 Blend the cornflour with a little water, then stir into the casserole. Cover and cook for 3 min, or until boiling. Sprinkle with parsley before serving. Alternatively serve topped with suet dumplings.

Suet dumplings *(serves 4–6)*

POWER LEVEL: 100% (FULL)
colour photograph above

100g (4oz) self-raising flour
$\frac{1}{2}$ × 5ml tsp ($\frac{1}{2}$ tsp) salt
50g (2oz) shredded suet
1–2 × 5ml tsp (1–2 tsp) dried mixed herbs, optional
cold water to mix

1 Sift the flour and salt. Stir in the suet, herbs and sufficient cold water to form a soft manageable dough.
2 Knead lightly and form into walnut size balls, rolling between the palms of the hands with a little extra flour if necessary.
3 Drop the dumplings onto the top of a hot, simmering casserole or stew in a deep, large dish. Cover and cook until light and well risen – about $4\frac{1}{2}$–5 min.

Suet Dumplings (below)

Suet crust pastry

225g (8oz) self-raising flour
pinch salt
100g (4oz) shredded suet
2–3 × 5ml tsp (2–3 tsp) dried mixed herbs, optional
150ml ($\frac{1}{4}$pt) cold water approximately

1 Sift the flour and salt, stir in the suet and herbs if used.
2 Mix in sufficient cold water to form a soft, manageable dough.
3 Knead lightly and use as required.

Aubergine with minced beef (serves 4–5)
POWER LEVEL: 100% (FULL)

75–100g (3–4oz) butter approximately
450g (1lb) aubergines, trimmed and sliced
1 onion, peeled and sliced
675g (1½lb) lean minced beef
150ml (¼pt) tomato purée
425ml (¾pt) beef stock
salt and freshly ground black pepper
For garnish:
chopped parsley

1 Melt the butter in a large bowl or dish for 2–2½ min. Add the aubergine slices, toss well in the butter. Cover and cook for 8–10 min until soft, stirring twice throughout.
2 Using a draining spoon, remove the aubergine slices onto a plate. Add the onion to the dish, with a little more butter if necessary; cover and cook for 4 min.
3 Add the minced beef, mix well with the onion, cover and cook for 6–7 min until browned, stirring once or twice and breaking down any lumps with a fork.
4 Add the tomato purée, stock and plenty of salt and pepper. Cover and cook for about 15 min until tender, stirring twice throughout.
5 Place a layer of aubergine at the bottom of a large serving dish and, using a draining spoon, arrange a layer of meat over the aubergine. Continue with the layers of aubergine and meat until all are used, ending with a layer of aubergine.
6 Pour over the sauce from the meat. Cover and cook for 5–6 min until heated through. Allow to stand for 2 min.
7 Serve hot sprinkled with plenty of freshly chopped parsley.

Moussaka (serves 4–6)
POWER LEVEL: 100% (FULL)

25g (1oz) butter
225g (8oz) onions, finely chopped
450g (1lb) minced lamb or beef
225g (8oz) tomatoes, skinned and chopped
2 × 15ml tbsp (2 tbsp) tomato purée
2 × 15ml tbsp (2 tbsp) stock or water
1 × 5ml tsp (1 tsp) salt
675g (1½lb) aubergines, thinly sliced
4 × 15ml tbsp (4 tbsp) white wine
1 egg, beaten
4 × 15ml tbsp (4 tbsp) grated parmesan cheese
275ml (½pt) white sauce (page 46)

1 Melt the butter in a casserole dish for 1 min. Add the onions to the butter and cook, uncovered, for 2 min. Add the meat, stir, and cook for 3–4 min.
2 Stir in the tomatoes, tomato purée, stock or water and salt.
3 Cook the aubergines (page 71)
4 Fill a large glass or pottery dish with alternate layers of meat mixture and the aubergines. Sprinkle the wine over the moussaka.
5 Add the beaten egg and half the cheese to the basic white sauce. Stir well and adjust seasoning to taste. Pour the sauce over the moussaka and sprinkle the rest of the cheese on top.
6 Cook, uncovered, for 20–25 min, turning the dish halfway through the cooking time.
7 Serve with a green or tomato and onion salad.

Note: *Cooked, sliced potatoes can be used instead of the aubergines if preferred.*

Pork with apricots and prunes (serves 4)
POWER LEVEL: 100% (FULL)

2 × 15ml tbsp (2 tbsp) oil
1 carrot, sliced
1 onion, chopped
450g (1lb) lean pork, diced
1 × 212g (7½oz) can apricots
1 × 212g (7½oz) can prunes
1 chicken stock cube
boiling water
1 × 15ml tbsp (1 tbsp) sherry
salt and black pepper
1 × 15ml tbsp (1 tbsp) cornflour

1 Heat the oil in a large, shallow casserole dish for 2 min. Add the prepared carrot and onion and cook for 3 min.
2 Add the pork, cook for 3 min, stir and cook for 2 min.
3 Drain the apricot and prune juices into a measuring jug. Add the stock cube and make the juices up to 550ml (1pt) with boiling water. Add the sherry.
4 Season the meat well, add the liquid and half the apricots and prunes. Cover and cook for 15 min. Stand for 10 min then cook for 10 min.
5 Blend the cornflour with a little water and stir into the casserole. Cook for 3 min, or until boiling.
6 Add the rest of the apricots and prunes. Cook for 2 min and adjust seasoning, if necessary, before serving.

Lamb with dill sauce (serves 4–6)
POWER LEVEL: 100% (FULL)

1½kg (3lb) leg of lamb
550ml (1pt) stock
2 onions, sliced
225g (8oz) carrots, peeled and sliced
salt and pepper
2 × 15ml tbsp (2 tbsp) dried dill

50g (2oz) butter
50g (2oz) plain flour
2 × 15ml tbsp (2 tbsp) white wine vinegar
1 × 15ml tbsp (1 tbsp) sugar
4 × 15ml tbsp (4 tbsp) single cream
1 egg yolk
1 × 15ml tbsp (1 tbsp) dried dill

1 Remove the meat from the bone and cut into 2cm (¾in) cubes. Place the meat in a casserole dish with the stock. Cover and cook for 5 min.
2 Add the prepared vegetables, seasoning and the 2 × 15ml tbsp (2 tbsp) dill. Cover and continue cooking for 10 min. Allow to stand for 10 min, then cook for a further 10 min. Drain and reserve the stock.
3 Melt the butter for 2 min, add the flour and gradually blend in the stock from the meat and vegetables.
4 Cook the sauce for 5 min, stirring 3 times during cooking. Add the vinegar and sugar and season to taste.
5 Blend together the cream and egg yolk and beat this into the sauce. Stir in the 1 × 15ml tbsp (1 tbsp) of dill.
6 Combine the sauce, meat and vegetables in the casserole, mixing thoroughly. Cover and reheat in the microwave for 5 min.

DO NOT FREEZE

Lamb portugaise (serves 4–6)
POWER LEVEL: 75%, 40% AND 100% (FULL)
colour page 57

1½kg (3lb) loin of lamb, boned
walnut stuffing
25g (1oz) butter
25g (1oz) plain flour
275ml (½pt) stock
1 × 15ml tbsp (1 tbsp) redcurrant jelly
juice ½ lemon
juice ½ orange
salt and pepper
1 × 15ml tbsp (1 tbsp) mint, chopped

1 Wipe the lamb with a damp cloth. Spread the stuffing over the meat, roll up and tie securely with string.
2 Score the surface of the lamb with a sharp knife.
3 Place the lamb in a large shallow dish and 'open' roast on 75% setting for 15 min, giving the dish a half turn at the end of the cooking period.
4 Reduce to 40% setting and cook for a further 20–30 min until cooked through, leave to stand.
5 Melt the butter in a bowl for 1 min on 100% (full) setting and blend in the flour.
6 Add the stock, jelly, fruit juices and seasonings,

gradually and stir until well blended.
7 Cook the sauce for 5 min on 100% (full) setting, stirring twice during the cooking time. Stir in the mint.
8 Slice the lamb, pour over a little of the sauce and serve the remainder separately.

Walnut stuffing
POWER LEVEL: 100% (FULL)

100g (4oz) walnuts
1 medium-sized onion
40g (1½oz) butter
40g (1½oz) breadcrumbs
1 × 15ml tbsp (1 tbsp) chopped parsley
1 × 5ml tsp (1 tsp) dried marjoram
½ lemon, grated rind and juice
1 egg, beaten
salt and pepper

1 Finely chop the walnuts and onion. Melt the butter in the microwave for 1 min. Add the onion and cook for 3 min.
2 Mix in the rest of the ingredients, using just enough beaten egg to bind the stuffing. Season well.
3 The stuffing can also be made by melting the butter for 1 min and then liquidising all the ingredients together. This gives a finely textured stuffing.

Spare ribs sweet and sour (serves 2–3)
POWER LEVEL: 100% (FULL)

675g (1½lb) spare rib chops
25g (1oz) butter
25g (1oz) onion, chopped
25g (1oz) plain flour
275ml (½pt) chicken stock, boiling
25g (1oz) green pepper, deseeded and chopped
3 × 15ml tbsp (3 tbsp) crushed pineapple
1 × 15ml tbsp (1 tbsp) wine vinegar
2 × 15ml tbsp (2 tbsp) worcestershire sauce
25g (1oz) soft brown sugar
1 × 15ml tbsp (1 tbsp) tomato purée
salt and pepper

1 Place the spare ribs in a large shallow dish. Cook for 3 min. Remove the chops from the dish and keep warm.
2 Melt the butter in the dish for 1 min. Add the onion and cook for 3 min. Stir in the flour, then add the stock gradually.
3 Stir in the remaining ingredients and mix well together.
4 Add the chops to the sauce. Cook, covered, for 5 min.
5 Turn the chops and stir the sauce, then return to the microwave and cook, uncovered, for 8–10 min.

Veal à la marengo (serves 4)

POWER LEVEL: 100% (FULL)

2 × 15ml tbsp (2 tbsp) oil
2 onions, thinly sliced
2 cloves garlic, finely chopped
675g (1½lb) stewing veal, diced
1 × 397g (14oz) can tomatoes
1 chicken stock cube
boiling water
2 × 15ml tbsp (2 tbsp) sherry
1 bay leaf
salt and pepper
100g (4oz) button mushrooms, sliced
1 × 5ml tsp (1 tsp) parsley, chopped

1 Heat the oil in a large casserole for 2 min. Add the onion and garlic and cook for 3 min. Add the meat and cook for 5 min.
2 Strain the juice from the tomatoes into a measuring jug. Add the stock cube and make the liquid up to 425ml (¾pt) with boiling water.
3 Put the tomatoes into the casserole, pour the stock over, then add the sherry, bay leaf and seasoning. Cover and cook for 20 min, stand for 10 min and stir well.
4 Cook for 10 min. Remove the bay leaf and add the mushrooms. Cover and cook for 5 min. Adjust seasoning, stir in the parsley and serve.

Quick poor man's cassoulet (serves 6–8)

POWER LEVEL: 100% (FULL)
colour page 23

40g (1½oz) lard
2 large cloves garlic, finely chopped
4 pork strips, boned, trimmed and diced
175–225g (6–8oz) stewing lamb, diced
150ml (¼pt) chicken stock
225g (8oz) garlic or pork sausage, cut into 1.5cm (½in) cubes
2 × 425g (15oz) cans baked beans
2 × 15ml tbsp (2 tbsp) brandy, optional
salt and pepper
For garnish:
1 × 15ml tbsp (1 tbsp) chopped parsley
For serving:
fresh bread or garlic bread (page 111)

1 Melt the lard in a large casserole for 2–3 min. Add the garlic and pork strips. Cook for 2 min, then add the lamb and stock and cook for 2 min.
2 Add the sausage, beans and brandy, if used. Season and stir well.
3 Cook for 10 min, stand for 5 min, cook for 10 min. Sprinkle with parsley before serving.
4 Serve hot with crusty fresh bread or garlic bread.

Crown roast of lamb (serves 4)

POWER LEVEL: 100% (FULL) OR 75%

2 best ends of lamb (5–6 cutlets each)
Orange and herb stuffing:
50g (2oz) butter
50g (2oz) onion, chopped
100g (4oz) fresh white breadcrumbs
1 orange, grated rind and juice
2 × 15ml tbsp (2 tbsp) fresh chopped herbs
or
1 × 15ml tbsp (1 tbsp) dried mixed herbs
seasoning
1 egg, beaten
For garnish:
cutlet frills
For serving:
glazed onions (page 78)

1 If you give the butcher sufficient notice, he will prepare the best ends of lamb by trimming away any excess fat and forming the two joints into a round or crown. Tie the crown securely with string.
2 Melt the butter for 1½ min on 100% (full) setting, toss the onion in the butter, cover and cook for a further 3 min. Add all the remaining ingredients for the stuffing and mix well together.
3 Place the meat onto a suitable cooking container and spoon the stuffing into the centre cavity. Allow 9 min per 450g (1lb) if using 100% (full) power or 11 min per 450g (1lb) if using a 75% setting.
4 Protect the tips of the cutlet bones with small smooth pieces of aluminium foil during the cooking time. Allow the joint to stand for 15–20 min halfway through the cooking time and a further 5–10 min at the end.
5 Place cutlet frills over the bones before serving the crown roast garnished with glazed onions.

Note: *Guard of Honour is prepared and cooked in a similar way except instead of the joints being formed into a crown, the best ends are placed back to back with the tips of the bones crossed like swords.*

Veal with aubergine (serves 4)

POWER LEVEL: 100% (FULL)
colour photograph opposite

4 veal escalopes, about 100g (4oz) each
few drops lemon juice
4 slices ham, about 25g (1oz) each
25g (1oz) butter
freshly ground black pepper
1 onion, peeled and thinly sliced
2–3 cloves garlic, crushed
450g (1lb) aubergines, trimmed and thinly sliced
4 tomatoes, skinned and quartered

1 × 15ml tbsp (1 tbsp) tomato purée
salt
1 glass white wine or stock
50g (2oz) cheddar cheese, grated
For garnish:
chopped parsley

1 Trim away any fat from the escalopes and beat into thin slices. Lay them out flat and sprinkle with a few drops of lemon juice.
2 Arrange a slice of ham on top of each escalope, then roll them up neatly and secure each one with a cocktail stick or tie with string.
3 Melt the butter in a large casserole for 1 min, arrange the veal rolls in the dish and turn or brush them with the butter. Sprinkle with black pepper.
4 Cover and cook for 8–10 min, turning the dish halfway through. Remove the veal rolls and keep warm.

Baked Avocados with Walnut Cheese (page 39), Veal with Aubergine (page 64) and Creamed Potatoes (page 76)

5 Add the onion to the butter and juices in the dish, cover and cook for 2 min. Add the garlic and aubergines, toss over well, cover and cook for 6–8 min or until tender.
6 Add the tomatoes, tomato purée, salt to taste and the wine or stock. Cover and cook for 3–4 min.
7 Remove the cocktail sticks or ties from the veal and replace the rolls in the dish on top of the aubergine mixture; sprinkle with the grated cheese and reheat for 2–3 min until the cheese is melted.
8 Serve hot sprinkled with plenty of chopped parsley. Plain boiled potatoes in their jackets go well with this dish.

65

Armenian lamb (*serves* 4)
POWER LEVEL: 100% (FULL)

1kg (2lb) fillet end leg of lamb
40g (1½oz) butter
2 medium-sized onions, chopped
1 clove garlic, chopped
25g (1oz) plain flour
1 × 5ml tsp (1 tsp) ground cumin seed
½ × 5ml tsp (½ tsp) ground allspice
2 × 15ml tbsp (2 tbsp) tomato purée
275ml (½pt) stock
salt and pepper
For serving:
rice pilaf (page 84)

1 Cut the meat from the bone and divide into small cubes, about 2cm (¾in) square.
2 Melt the butter in a dish for 2 min, add the onion and garlic, cook for 3 min. Add the meat to the onion and garlic and cook, covered, for 2 min.
3 Add all the other ingredients. Cook, covered, for 10 min, stand for 15 min, cook for 5 min.
4 Serve with rice pilaf.

Carbonnade of beef (*serves* 4)
POWER LEVEL: 100% (FULL) AND 75%

50g (2oz) butter
3 large onions, thinly sliced
675g (1½lb) braising steak, cut into 2.5cm (1in) cubes
1 × 15ml tbsp (1 tbsp) seasoned flour
50g (2oz) streaky bacon, diced
275ml (½pt) brown ale
boiling stock
salt and pepper
bouquet garni
1 × 5ml tsp (1 tsp) french mustard
15g (½oz) cornflour
For serving:
crusty french bread

1 Melt the butter in a large casserole dish for 1½ min on 100% (full) setting. Add the onions and cook for 4 min.
2 Toss the meat in the seasoned flour.
3 Add the bacon to the onions, cook for 1 min on 100% (full) setting, add the meat, cook for a further 2 min.
4 Stir in the brown ale and sufficient stock to cover the meat. Add the seasonings, bouquet garni and mustard.
5 Cover and cook on 75% setting for 40–50 min, stirring occasionally.
6 Leave the casserole to cool.
7 Remove the bouquet garni and adjust seasonings.
8 Blend the cornflour with a little of the cooking liquor and stir into the casserole.
9 Reheat on 100% (full) setting for 3–4 min, stirring every 2 min until heated through and thickened.
10 Serve with crusty french bread.

Hungarian goulash (*serves* 4)
POWER LEVEL: 100% (FULL) AND 50% (DEFROST)

450g (1lb) stewing steak, cut into small cubes
3 × 15ml tbsp (3 tbsp) seasoned flour
25ml (1fl oz) oil
2 medium-sized onions, chopped
1 green pepper, deseeded and chopped
2 × 5ml tsp (2 tsp) paprika pepper
3 × 5ml tsp (3 tsp) tomato purée
pinch grated nutmeg
salt and pepper
50g (2oz) plain flour
275–425ml (½–¾pt) boiling stock
2 tomatoes, skinned and quartered
bouquet garni
For serving:
boiled rice or pasta shells (page 81)

1 Toss the meat in the seasoned flour. Heat the oil in a large dish for 1–2 min on 100% (full) setting.
2 Stir in the meat then add all the other ingredients, blending well.
3 Cover and cook for 10–14 min on 100% (full) setting, stand for 10 min, then cook for 20 min on 50% (defrost) setting, stirring twice throughout.
4 Remove bouquet garni and serve hot with boiled rice or pasta shells.

Chicken with peanuts (*serves* 4)
POWER LEVEL: 100% (FULL)

4 chicken joints
2 × 15ml tbsp (2 tbsp) seasoned flour
2 × 15ml tbsp (2 tbsp) oil
1 onion, chopped
150ml (¼pt) milk
150ml (¼pt) stock
1 × 15ml tbsp (1 tbsp) peanut butter
1 × 15ml tbsp (1 tbsp) cornflour
2 × 15ml tbsp (2 tbsp) single cream
salt and pepper
For garnish:
50g (2oz) salted peanuts

1 Toss the chicken joints in the seasoned flour. Heat the oil in a large dish for 1 min, add the onion and cook, covered, for 3 min.
2 Add the chicken joints, flesh side downwards, and cook, uncovered, for 3 min. Turn the joints over and cook for 2 min.

3 Mix the milk, stock and peanut butter in a small bowl and heat for 2 min. Pour over the chicken joints, cover and cook for 15 min. Turn the dish every 5 min.

4 Remove the chicken pieces and blend the cornflour with a little of the sauce. Stir the cornflour into the liquid and cook for 4 min, stirring every minute. Add the cream and seasoning and mix well.

5 Return the chicken to the dish, spooning the sauce over the joints. Reheat in the microwave for 3 min. Sprinkle with the peanuts and serve immediately.

DO NOT FREEZE

Mexican chicken (serves 4)
POWER LEVEL: 100% (FULL)

25g (1oz) butter
1 green pepper, deseeded and sliced
1 red pepper, deseeded and sliced
2 medium-sized onions, chopped
2 cloves garlic, crushed
salt and pepper
1 × 396g (14oz) can tomatoes
2 × 15ml tbsp (2 tbsp) tomato purée
4 chicken portions
100g (4oz) sweetcorn
100g (4oz) mushrooms, washed and sliced
4 × 15ml tbsp (4 tbsp) single cream
For garnish:
2 × 15ml tbsp (2 tbsp) chopped parsley

1 Melt the butter in a large casserole dish for 1 min.

2 Add the peppers, onions, garlic and seasoning, then cover with clingfilm and cook for 3 min. Mix the tomatoes and tomato purée into the pepper mixture.

3 Season the chicken joints lightly and add to the pepper mixture. Cover and cook for 15 min.

4 Add the sweetcorn and mushrooms and cook, still covered, for a further 15–20 min.

5 Remove the chicken joints from the casserole. Stir the cream into the sauce and return the chicken to the casserole dish. Sprinkle with parsley before serving.

Cottage pie (serves 4–6)
POWER LEVEL: 100% (FULL)
colour page 49

25g (1oz) butter or margarine
1 small onion, finely chopped
450g (1lb) minced beef
25g (1oz) flour
150ml ($\frac{1}{4}$pt) beef stock
1 × 5ml tsp (1 tsp) chopped parsley
salt and freshly ground black pepper
1 × 5ml tsp (1 tsp) worcestershire sauce

450g (1lb) creamed potatoes (page 76)
knob butter
paprika pepper for sprinkling

1 Melt the butter or margarine in a large round casserole for 1 min. Add the onion and cook for 2–3 min.

2 Add the minced beef, mix with the onion, cover and cook for 5–6 min until browned, stirring once or twice and breaking down any lumps with a fork.

3 Stir in the flour, stock, parsley, seasoning and worcestershire sauce. Cover and cook for 10–15 min, until tender, stirring every 5 min.

4 Wipe the sides of the dish and cover the meat with the potato, marking the surface with a fork. Alternatively, pipe the potato over the top using a large star nozzle fitted into a forcing bag.

5 Top with slivers of butter and cook until hot through (1–2 min if the ingredients are still hot, 5–6 min if cool). Sprinkle with paprika or brown the top under a hot grill.

Duck in orange and ginger sauce (serves 4)
POWER LEVEL: 100% (FULL)

1 × 15ml tbsp (1 tbsp) oil
1 onion, chopped
4 portions duckling
2 oranges
1 chicken stock cube
boiling water
3 × 15ml tbsp (3 tbsp) clear honey
1$\frac{1}{2}$ × 5ml tsp (1$\frac{1}{2}$ tsp) ground ginger
salt and pepper
1 bay leaf
1 × 15ml tbsp (1 tbsp) cornflour

1 Heat the oil in a large casserole dish for 1 min. Add the onions, cover and cook for 3 min.

2 Add the duck portions, cover and cook for 5 min.

3 Grate the rind from the oranges. Squeeze the juice from 1$\frac{1}{2}$ of the oranges. Add the stock cube and make the juice up to 550ml (1pt) with boiling water.

4 Add the honey, ginger and seasoning to the liquid, then pour over the duck. Sprinkle the orange rind over the duck and add the bay leaf.

5 Cover and cook for 20 min, stand for 10 min, cook for 10–15 min.

6 Blend the cornflour with a little water. Remove the duck portions from the casserole. Stir the cornflour into the sauce after skimming off the surplus fat and removing the bay leaf. Cook for 3 min or until boiling. Stir well.

7 Return the duck to the sauce and reheat for 2 min. Before serving, garnish with orange slices from the remaining $\frac{1}{2}$ orange.

Lamb casserole with leeks (serves 4–6)
POWER LEVEL: 100% (FULL) AND 30%

675g (1½lb) chops, middle or best end of neck
3 leeks, coarsely sliced
1 × 425g (15oz) can tomatoes
275ml (½pt) stock or water
1 × 15ml tbsp (1 tbsp) tomato purée
½ × 5ml tsp (½ tsp) dried oregano
2 × 5ml tsp (2 tsp) dried mixed herbs
1 × 5 ml tsp (1 tsp) salt
freshly ground black pepper
For garnish:
freshly chopped parsley

1 Arrange the chops and leeks in a large, shallow casserole dish.
2 Mix the remaining ingredients together in a large bowl, cook for 4–5 min on 100% (full) setting and pour over the chops and leeks.
3 Cook on 100% (full) setting for 15 min, give the dish a half turn.
4 Reduce to 30% setting and cook for a further 20–30 min.
5 Serve hot sprinkled with parsley.

Chilli con carne (serves 4–6)
POWER LEVEL: 100% (FULL)

2 × 15ml tbsp (2 tbsp) oil
2 large onions, finely chopped
450g (1lb) minced beef
2 × 15ml tbsp (2 tbsp) tomato purée
1–2 × 15ml tbsp (1–2 tbsp) chilli powder
1 × 5ml tsp (1 tsp) paprika
salt and pepper
1 × 397g (14oz) can kidney beans
For serving:
boiled rice (page 81)

1 Heat the oil in a large bowl for 2 min. Add the onions and cook for 3 min. Add the meat and mix well.
2 Cover and cook for 2 min, stir, cook for 2 min. Add the tomato purée and seasonings, mixing well.
3 Drain the kidney beans, reserving the juice and making up to 225ml (8fl oz) with water. Add the liquid to the meat.
4 Cover and cook for 10 min, stand for 5 min. Stir in the kidney beans, then cook for 5–10 min. Skim off the surplus fat and adjust the seasoning before serving.

Chicken and sweetcorn oatie pie (serves 4)
POWER LEVEL: 100% (FULL)

1 × 5ml tsp (1 tsp) cornflour
150ml (¼pt) chicken stock, approximately
225g (8oz) cooked chicken, roughly chopped
325g (11½oz) can sweetcorn
salt and freshly ground black pepper
100g (4oz) plain flour
pinch salt
50g (2oz) rolled oats
75g (3oz) butter or margarine

1 Lightly grease a large ovenware pie dish.
2 Blend the cornflour with a little of the stock, add the rest and cook for 1½–2 min, stirring every minute until thickened.
3 Add the chicken and the sweetcorn. Mix together, add seasoning to taste and a little extra stock if necessary to moisten. Place the mixture into the prepared pie dish.
4 Sift the flour and salt. Stir in the rolled oats and rub in the butter to form a coarse crumb mixture. Sprinkle over the chicken and sweetcorn.
5 Cook for 8–10 min until hot through and topping is cooked, giving a quarter turn every 2 min. Serve hot.

Turkey meat loaf
POWER LEVEL: 100% (FULL)

450g (1lb) cooked turkey meat
1 large onion
100g (4oz) breadcrumbs
3 × 15ml tbsp (3 tbsp) tomato purée
4 eggs
½ × 5ml tsp (½ tsp) allspice
pinch nutmeg
salt and pepper

1 Mince the meat and onion together and place in a large mixing bowl. Add all the other ingredients and mix thoroughly.
2 Press the mixture into a rectangular dish and cook in the microwave for 12–15 min. Turn the dish every 5 min and allow 5 min standing time halfway through cooking.
3 Serve hot with vegetables or cold with salad.

Note: *Cooked ham or chicken can be used as alternatives to the turkey.*

Vegetables

Fresh vegetables cooked in the microwave are delicious and retain their full flavour, colour and nutritional value as they are cooked in their own juices, requiring very little additional liquid. In fact some vegetables – spinach and spring greens, for example – are cooked using only the water which clings to the leaves after washing. Roasting bags and boiling bags are ideal for cooking vegetables as they can be easily shaken or turned over to stir the contents during the cooking cycle. Remember, however, that the wire ties supplied with some makes must not be used; rubber bands or string ties make suitable alternatives and the bag should be tied loosely to allow some steam to escape. Vegetables will remain hot for a considerable time after cooking if the bag is not opened. It is, therefore, possible to cook several varieties of vegetables one after another and serve them together.

If preferred, vegetables may be cooked using more water in a casserole dish, covered with a lid or clingfilm, but the cooking time should be increased to allow for the extra volume in the oven. It is not always quicker to cook vegetables by microwave than cooking conventionally, but the results are well worthwhile.

Blanching vegetables

It is possible to blanch vegetables for the freezer in the

Green Beans Italian Style (page 78), Broad Beans with Ham (page 74) and French Bean Salad (page 76)

microwave oven but only attempt small quantities at a time. Some vegetables are more successful and will keep a better colour than others.

The vegetables should be prepared for blanching in the normal way, placed in a large covered casserole with water allowing 75–100ml (3–4fl oz) per 450g (1lb) vegetables, depending on the type – for example, sliced runner beans would require slightly less water than cauliflower florets.

The vegetables should be cooked for half the recommended cooking time given on the vegetable cooking chart, but it is important to shake or stir them at least once during the blanching period. After blanching, cool the vegetables in iced water, then pack and freeze in the normal way.

Vegetables may be blanched in boiling bags for convenience, with very little water – about as much as recommended when cooking vegetables. To blanch them, cook in the microwave for half the recommended cooking time, shaking them frequently throughout. Chill them by plunging the whole package up to the opening in a bowl of iced water; this will reduce the temperature and expel the air at the same time, automatically creating a vacuum pack for the freezer. Seal the bag in the normal way and freeze.

Home-frozen vegetables when required for use should be cooked for the full time recommended for fresh vegetables but allow an extra 1–3 min if using them straight from the freezer, when no extra water will be required.

Frozen vegetables

Commercially frozen products may cook quicker than home-frozen ones. This is due to the fact that commercial freezing takes place at very high speed

and, as a result, the ice crystals are smaller and melt more quickly during cooking. The times given in the following charts are approximate, as the type and size of the container and the freezing method used will affect the cooking time required. Also the degree of cooking is a personal choice – some may prefer crispier vegetables, while others prefer them cooked a little longer. Adjust the cooking times to suit your own individual requirements.

Frozen vegetables are defrosted and cooked in one operation, using 100% (full) setting.

Canned vegetables

Most canned vegetables are cooked during the processing and, therefore, only need reheating in the microwave. The food must be removed from the can and placed in a suitable covered container. Heat on 100% (full) setting for 3–4 min for the 400–425g (14–15oz) size and for 2–2½ min for the 200–225g (7–8oz) size. Stir the contents of the dish halfway through the cooking time to ensure even heating.

Points to remember

1 Do not overseason the vegetables as it can have a toughening effect. If in doubt, adjust the seasoning after cooking.
2 The times given are approximate as the age and the thickness of the vegetables will affect cooking time. Therefore, test regularly during cooking.
3 If the quantity given on the chart is altered, the time should be adjusted accordingly. Allow about $\frac{1}{3}$–$\frac{1}{2}$ extra time if doubling the quantity of vegetables to be cooked.
4 Do not overcook as the vegetables will continue to cook for a short while after they are removed from the oven due to the heat retained.
5 Vegetables cooked in their skins, ie jacket potatoes and whole tomatoes, should be pricked well to prevent them bursting during the cooking process.
6 When 'boiling' potatoes it is usually better to cook them in their skins with a little added water as described previously and to remove the skins, if required, after cooking. Some kinds of potatoes cook extremely well either scraped or peeled but certain varieties tend to turn black during cooking in the microwave.
7 When cooking an item such as a jacket potato, one potato weighing 100–150g (4–5oz) will take 5–6 min, two will take 7–9 min and three will take 10–11 min and so on.

| Vegetable | Cooking time | |
	225g (½lb)	450g (1lb)
asparagus	6–7 min	10–11 min
beans, broad	7–8 min	10–11 min
beans, french or runner	7–8 min	10–11 min
broccoli	6–8 min	8–10 min
cabbage	6–7 min	10–11 min
carrots	6–8 min	9–10 min
cauliflower florets	4–6 min	7–9 min
corn kernels	3–4 min	7–8 min
corn on the cob	4–5 min	7–8 min
	(1 cob)	(2 cobs)
courgettes	4–5 min	6–8 min
peas	4–5 min	8–9 min
spinach, chopped or leaf	7–8 min	10–11 min
stewpack	6–8 min	9–11 min
swedes or turnips	7–8 min	10–12 min
vegetables mixed, diced	5–6 min	7–9 min

Vegetable cooking chart

Vegetable and quantity	Preparation	Amount of salted water to be added	Cooking time in mins 100% (full)
artichokes	see recipes		
asparagus 225g (8oz)	trim and leave whole	2 × 15ml tbsp (2 tbsp)	thin spears 6–8 thick spears 8–10
aubergines 450g (1lb)	wash, slice, sprinkle with salt and leave for 30 min, rinse	2 × 15ml tbsp (2 tbsp)	8–10
beans, broad 450g (1lb)	remove from pods	3 × 15ml tbsp (3 tbsp)	8–10
beans, french 450g (1lb)	wash and cut	2 × 15ml tbsp (2 tbsp)	8–10
beans, runner 450g (1lb)	string and slice	2 × 15ml tbsp (2 tbsp)	8–10
beetroot 450g (1lb) 225g (8oz) whole	peel and slice prick skin, wrap in clingfilm	2 × 15ml tbsp (2 tbsp)	7–8 12–15
broccoli 450g (1lb)	trim, cut into spears	2 × 15ml tbsp (2 tbsp)	8–12
brussels sprouts 450g (1lb)	wash, remove outer leaves and trim	2 × 15ml tbsp (2 tbsp)	8–10
cabbage 450g (1lb)	wash and shred finely	2 × 15ml tbsp (2 tbsp)	8–10
carrots 225g (8oz)	*new* wash, scrape and cut into strips or leave whole, depending on size *old* scrape or peel and slice	2 × 15ml tbsp (2 tbsp) ,,	7–10 7–10
cauliflower 675g (1½lb) 450g (1lb) whole	wash and cut into florets trim outside leaves, wash	4 × 15ml tbsp (4 tbsp) ,,	10–11 10–11
celery 350g (12oz)	wash, trim and slice	3 × 15ml tbsp (3 tbsp)	10–12
corn on the cob 2 × 225g (8oz)	wash and trim	4 × 15ml tbsp (4 tbsp) *or* 40g (1½oz) butter	6–8
courgettes 450g (1lb)	wash, trim and slice	—	8–10
leeks 450g (1lb)	wash, trim and slice	2 × 15ml tbsp (2 tbsp)	7–10
marrow 450g (1lb)	peel, cut into 2cm (¾in) rings, remove seeds and quarter the rings	2 × 15ml tbsp (2 tbsp)	8–10
mushrooms 225g (8oz)	peel or wipe or wash	2 × 15ml tbsp (2 tbsp) of stock *or* 25g (1oz) butter	5–6
okra 450g (1lb)	wash, trim, sprinkle with salt, leave for 30 min, rinse	2 × 15ml tbsp (2 tbsp) *or* 25g (1oz) butter or oil	8–10

onions 225g (8oz)	peel and slice	2 × 15ml tbsp (2 tbsp) *or* 25g (1oz) butter or oil	5–7
parsnips 450g (1lb)	peel and slice	2 × 15ml tbsp (2 tbsp)	8–10
peas 225g (8oz)	remove from pods	2 × 15ml tbsp (2 tbsp)	8–10
potatoes, new, in their jackets 450g (1lb)	wash thoroughly	2 × 15ml tbsp (2 tbsp)	10–12
potatoes, old, in their jackets 450g (1lb)	wash and scrub thoroughly, dry and prick skins	—	10–12
spinach 450g (1lb)	break up thicker stalks, wash thoroughly	—	6–8
spring greens 450g (1lb)	break up thicker stalks, wash and shred	2 × 15ml tbsp (2 tbsp)	8–10
swedes 450g (1lb)	peel and dice	2 × 15ml tbsp (2 tbsp)	6–7
tomatoes 450g (1lb)	wash and halve, place in shallow dish and cover with lid or clingfilm	—	6–8
turnips 450g (1lb)	peel and dice	2 × 15ml tbsp (2 tbsp)	8–10

Dried vegetables

Dried peas, beans and lentils – pulses – require soaking before cooking conventionally or by microwave. They should be soaked in cold water for 8–12 hours, or overnight if possible. Alternatively, cover them with cold water and bring to the boil in the microwave, cook for 2–3 min, then allow them to stand for 1–1½ hours to swell and soften. Drain and rinse well.

To cook, place the pulses in a large container, ensuring that there is sufficient room for the water to boil during cooking. Cover with boiling water from the kettle and bring the dish to the boil in the microwave cooker. Lentils take approximately 20–25 min to cook and larger pulses 40–60 min. All pulses should be covered during the cooking period. Be prepared to top up the cooking water with extra boiling water from the kettle when necessary.

Drying herbs

Preserving herbs by drying in the microwave is very quick and easy compared with conventional methods and the microwave cooker dries small quantities very successfully. Many varieties of herbs are annual plants and, when near the end of their season, it is possible to dry them by microwave to last through the winter months. The method is simple and the results are excellent, retaining better colours and aromas than conventionally dried herbs.

It is preferable if the herbs are clean and dry when picked, otherwise wash them thoroughly and pat them dry between pieces of kitchen paper towel. Gently squeeze as much moisture as possible from them after washing as this will help to cut down the drying time and give better results. Remove the leaves from the stems and measure about 1 cupful of the leaves. Spread the herbs out evenly onto two thicknesses of kitchen paper towel placed on the microwave cooker shelf and cover with two more pieces of kitchen paper towel. This helps to absorb moisture during the heating process.

Heat on 100% (full) setting for 4–6 min, turning the kitchen paper towels with the herbs once. Check after minimum time – when dry, the herbs will be brittle and break very easily. Leave to cool between the kitchen paper towels before crushing and storing in an airtight jar which should be kept in a cool, dry place.

Almondine Potatoes (page 76) and Creamed Mushrooms and Peas (page 79)

Tomato and Mushroom Crumble (page 76) and Baked Stuffed Tomatoes (page 38)

Broad beans with ham (serves 4–6)

POWER LEVEL: 50% (DEFROST) AND 100% (FULL)
colour page 69

450g (1lb) shelled broad beans
2 × 15ml tbsp) salted water
275ml (½pt) béchamel sauce (page 46)
2 × 15ml tbsp (2 tbsp) cream
225g (8oz) lean cooked ham, shredded
1 × 15ml tbsp (1 tbsp) freshly chopped parsley

1 Cook the broad beans with the salted water in a suitable covered container for 8–10 min on 100% (full) setting. After cooking, if the beans are old, remove the thin skins.
2 Add the beans to the sauce with the cream and ham. Cook for a further 2–3 min until heated through, but do not allow to boil.
3 Stir in the chopped parsley and serve.

Note: *225–350g (8–12oz) butter beans, soaked and cooked (page 72) or canned butter beans, can be used instead of broad beans for this dish.*

Broccoli in butter sauce (serves 4)

POWER LEVEL: 100% (FULL)

The green broccoli, or calabrese, contrasts well with the creamy white sauce. Serve as a starter or as a special vegetable dish with the main course.

450g (1lb) green broccoli, washed and trimmed
4 × 15ml tbsp (4 tbsp) salted water
For the sauce:
50g (2oz) butter
2 × 5ml tsp (2 tsp) plain flour
1 egg yolk
juice of half a lemon
2 × 15ml tbsp (2 tbsp) double cream
salt and pepper

1 Place the broccoli in a casserole dish with the salted water. Cover and cook for 8–12 min. (Cooking times will vary with the size of the broccoli heads.) Allow to stand for a few minutes, then drain and reserve the cooking liquor. Keep the broccoli warm.
2 Melt the butter for 1–2 min, stir in the flour and blend well together. Stir in the broccoli cooking liquid. Heat for 2–3 min until thickened.
3 Beat the egg yolk with the lemon juice and some of the hot sauce. Blend well together and add to the sauce, beating well.
4 Stir in the cream and heat for 15–30 sec, but do not allow the sauce to boil. Adjust the seasoning.
5 Pour the sauce over the broccoli in the dish and serve immediately.

DO NOT FREEZE

Braised celery (serves 4)

POWER LEVEL: 100% (FULL)

25g (1oz) butter
2 rashers bacon
1 small onion, peeled and finely chopped
350g (12oz) celery, cut into 7.5cm (3in) strips
275ml (½pt) boiling chicken stock
salt and pepper

1 Melt the butter for 1 min in a shallow dish.
2 Remove the rind from the rashers and cut them into strips.
3 Add the bacon strips and the chopped onion to the butter, toss well, cover and cook for 2 min.
4 Add the celery and cook for 2 min.
5 Pour on the stock, add the seasonings, cover and cook for 15–20 min.
6 Serve hot.

Stuffed cabbage leaves (serves 4)

POWER LEVEL: 100% (FULL) AND 50% (DEFROST)
colour page 41

This is a good way of using up left-over cold meats and makes a substantial main course.

8 large cabbage leaves, trimmed and washed
2 × 15ml tbsp (2 tbsp) salted water
25g (1oz) butter
1 large onion, peeled and finely chopped
350g (12oz) cooked chicken or ham, minced
1 × 15ml tbsp (1 tbsp) chopped parsley
4 × 15ml tbsp (4 tbsp) fresh white breadcrumbs
200–225g (7–8oz) can tomatoes
salt and freshly ground black pepper
For serving:
tomato sauce (page 47)

1 Place the cabbage leaves with the salted water in a boiling or roasting bag and cook on 100% (full) setting for 4–5 min. Drain well.
2 Melt the butter for 1 min on 100% (full) setting, add the onion, toss well, cover and cook for a further 5–6 min until transparent and soft.
3 Stir in the minced cooked chicken or ham, parsley and breadcrumbs.
4 Drain the tomatoes and reserve the juice. Add the tomatoes to the meat mixture with sufficient of the juice to moisten. Add salt and pepper to taste.
5 Divide the mixture between the cabbage leaves then roll up each one into a parcel and secure with a cocktail stick or tie with string.
6 Place the stuffed cabbage leaves in a buttered serving dish, cover and cook on 50% (defrost) setting for 8–10 min until heated through.
7 Serve hot with tomato sauce.

German red cabbage (*serves 4–6*)
POWER LEVEL: 100% (FULL)
colour page 83

450g (1lb) red cabbage, very finely shredded
50g (2oz) butter, melted
1 large onion, peeled and sliced
2 cloves garlic, finely chopped
1 cooking apple, peeled and sliced
1 bay leaf
pinch each dried parsley and thyme
pinch each ground cinnamon and nutmeg
salt and freshly ground black pepper
1 orange, grated rind
2 × 15ml tbsp (2 tbsp) brown sugar
1 × 5ml tsp (1 tsp) caraway seeds
1 small wine glass red wine

1 Toss the shredded cabbage in the melted butter, cover and cook for 3–4 min.
2 Add all the other ingredients and stir well. Cover and cook for 20–25 min, stirring 2–3 times throughout.
3 Remove the bay leaf and serve hot.

Mushrooms au gratin (*serves 4*)
POWER LEVEL: 100% (FULL)

25g (1oz) butter
450g (1lb) button mushrooms, washed and sliced
salt and pepper
275ml ($\frac{1}{2}$pt) béchamel sauce (page 46)
150ml ($\frac{1}{4}$pt) single cream
3 × 15ml tbsp (3 tbsp) browned breadcrumbs
3 × 15ml tbsp (3 tbsp) grated cheddar and parmesan cheese, mixed

1 Melt the butter in a serving dish for 1 min. Add the mushrooms, season lightly, cover and cook for 5 min; leave to stand for a few minutes.
2 Heat the béchamel sauce, if necessary, then stir in the cream.
3 Drain the mushrooms and spoon the sauce over the mushrooms. Mix the breadcrumbs with the cheese and sprinkle over the top of the sauce. Heat in the microwave for 2–3 min until the cheese is melted. Alternatively, brown under a hot grill.
4 Serve immediately.

FREEZE THE SAUCE SEPARATELY. FINISH WITH THE BREADCRUMBS AND CHEESE JUST BEFORE SERVING

Almondine potatoes

colour page 73

Follow the method and ingredients for creamed potatoes, omitting the milk but stirring in the butter and seasonings to taste. Allow the mixture to cool then refrigerate until cold. Divide the mixture into 8 portions and roll into balls, shaped between the palms of the hands, using a little flour, if necessary, to prevent the potatoes from sticking. Roll the potato balls in finely chopped and toasted almonds. Place on the microwave cooker shelf or in a serving dish and heat through uncovered for about 3 min.

Tomato and mushroom crumble

(serves 4–6)
POWER LEVEL: 100% (FULL)
colour page 73

550ml (1pt) tomato sauce (page 47)
225g (8oz) mushrooms, washed and sliced
75g (3oz) wholemeal flour
75g (3oz) plain flour
$\frac{1}{2}$ × 5ml tsp ($\frac{1}{2}$ tsp) salt
$\frac{1}{2}$ × 5ml tsp ($\frac{1}{2}$ tsp) dry mustard
75g (3oz) butter or margarine
75g (3oz) cheese, finely grated
For garnish:
tomato slices

1 Lightly grease a large round ovenware dish.
2 Mix the tomato sauce with the sliced mushrooms and place in the greased dish.
3 Sift the flours with the salt and mustard and rub in the butter or margarine finely. Stir in the grated cheese.
4 Sprinkle the crumble topping lightly over the tomato and mushroom mixture and smooth the top.
5 Cook for 8–10 min, giving a quarter turn every 2 min until hot through and the crumble is cooked.
6 Serve hot garnished with tomato slices.

Creamed potatoes *(serves 4)*
POWER LEVEL: 100% (FULL)
colour page 65

450g (1lb) potatoes, washed
2 × 15ml tbsp (2 tbsp) salted water
75–125ml (3–4fl oz) milk
25g (1oz) butter
salt and pepper

1 Prick the skins of the potatoes with a fork. Place with the salted water in a casserole dish, cover and cook for 10–12 min or until tender. Test with a fork.
2 Drain the potatoes, remove the skins or cut in half

and scoop out the potato from the skins.
3 Mash the potatoes with a fork or potato masher.
4 Heat the milk for 1 min and add to the potatoes with the butter and seasoning.
5 Beat well together and serve hot.

French bean salad *(serves 4–6)*
POWER LEVEL: 100% (FULL)
colour page 69

French beans, lightly cooked and served cold, make an excellent ingredient for a mixed salad, or are delicious served on their own with a plain dressing.

450g (1lb) french beans, trimmed and left whole
2 × 15ml tbsp (2 tbsp) salted water
6 × 15ml tbsp (6 tbsp) olive oil
2 × 15ml tbsp (2 tbsp) lemon juice or wine vinegar
salt and freshly ground black pepper
pinch sugar
For garnish:
1 hardboiled egg

1 Wash the beans and place them with the salted water in a serving dish. Cover and cook for 6 min, shaking or stirring the beans twice throughout. Leave to stand for a few minutes. The beans should be crisp.
2 Whisk the olive oil, lemon juice or wine vinegar, seasoning and sugar together.
3 Drain the beans, add the dressing and allow to cool.
4 When cold, toss the beans in the dressing.
5 Separate the egg white from the yolk. Chop the white finely and rub the yolk through a sieve.
6 Garnish the beans attractively with the egg yolk and white and serve.

DO NOT FREEZE

Fried onions *(serves 3–4)*
POWER LEVEL: 100% (FULL)

2 large onions, peeled and finely sliced
3 × 15ml tbsp (3 tbsp) oil or dripping
caster sugar for dusting

1 Push the onion slices through to form rings.
2 Heat the oil or dripping for 2–3 min in a large bowl. Toss in the onion rings so that they are well coated in the oil.
3 Cover and cook for 5 min, stir well and dust with a little caster sugar. Cover and cook for 3–4 min until tender.
4 Serve hot with sausages or steaks.

Note: *Alternatively, the onions may be cooked in a browning dish which has been preheated for 5 min. Add the onion rings which have been tossed in the oil or dripping, cover and cook for 6–7 min, tossing the onions over once halfway through.*

Pissaladière with Garlic Bread (below)

Pissaladière (*serves 6*)

POWER LEVEL: 100% (FULL) AND 75%
colour photograph above

This strongly flavoured tart is characteristic of dishes from southern France and is similar to the Italian pizza but with a lighter pastry base. It makes a substantial lunch or supper dish served on its own or with crusty bread.

175g (6oz) rich shortcrust pastry (page 32)
3 × 15ml tbsp (3 tbsp) olive oil
2 large onions, peeled and finely sliced
1–2 cloves garlic, crushed or finely chopped
225g (8oz) can tomatoes
1 × 15ml tbsp (1 tbsp) tomato purée
2 × 5ml tsp (2 tsp) mixed chopped herbs, eg basil, oregano, thyme
salt and freshly ground black pepper
1 × 5ml tsp (1 tsp) caster sugar
50g (2oz) can anchovy fillets
50–75g (2–3oz) black olives
For serving:
crusty french bread or garlic bread (page 111)

1 Roll out the pastry, line a 20cm (8in) flan dish and bake blind (page 32).
2 Place the oil, onions and garlic into a large bowl and toss well. Cover and cook on 100% (full) setting for 5–6 min until the onions are soft and transparent. Shake or stir twice throughout. Drain off the liquid.
3 Roughly chop the tomatoes and place in a bowl with the tomato purée, herbs, seasoning and sugar. Stir and boil in the microwave on 100% (full) setting until the liquid quantity is reduced and the mixture is fairly thick.
4 Add the tomato mixture to the drained onions and pour into the pastry case.
5 Drain the anchovy fillets and cut in half lengthwise. Arrange over the top of the flan in a lattice design. Garnish with the olives.
6 Cook on 75% setting for 8–10 min until heated through thoroughly. Alternatively, heat through on 100% (full) setting for 3 min, allow to stand for 3 min, repeat until hot through.
7 Serve hot with crusty french bread or garlic bread.

77

Mediterranean stuffed aubergines (*serves 4–6*)

POWER LEVEL: 100% (FULL)

2 medium-sized aubergines
salt for sprinkling
2 × 15ml tbsp (2 tbsp) oil
1 onion, finely chopped
½ green pepper, finely chopped
2 cloves garlic, finely chopped
225g (8oz) mince
4 tomatoes, skinned and chopped
1 courgette, trimmed, halved and thinly sliced
2 × 15ml tbsp (2 tbsp) tomato purée
1 × 5ml tsp (1 tsp) oregano
salt and black pepper to taste
For garnish:
grated parmesan cheese

1 Trim the aubergines. Cut into 8 thick slices, sprinkle with salt and heat in the microwave for 3 min. Leave to stand for 10–15 min. Wash thoroughly in cold water.
2 Remove the centre of the aubergines and reserve. Place the aubergine rings in an ovenware serving dish.
3 Heat the oil in a mixing bowl for 2 min. Add the onion, pepper and garlic and cook for 3 min. Add the meat and cook for 4 min.
4 Chop the reserved aubergine centres and stir into the meat mixture along with the rest of the ingredients. Cover the bowl with clingfilm and cook for 5 min, stand for 5 min.
5 Cover and cook the aubergine rings, in the serving dish, for 4–5 min. Stuff the rings with the filling. Cover and cook for 3 min. Sprinkle with parmesan cheese before serving.

Green beans Italian style (*serves 4*)

POWER LEVEL: 100% (FULL)
colour page 69

Runner or french beans can be used for this dish – a good way of serving beans towards the end of their season.

450g (1lb) runner or french beans, prepared and sliced thickly
2 × 15ml tbsp (2 tbsp) salted water
40g (1½oz) butter
1–2 × 15ml tbsp (1–2 tbsp) olive oil
2 × 5ml tsp (2 tsp) freshly chopped parsley or sage
1–2 cloves garlic, crushed
salt and freshly ground black pepper
2–3 × 5ml tsp (2–3 tsp) parmesan cheese, grated
For garnish:
freshly chopped herbs

1 Wash the beans and place with the salted water in

a serving dish, cover and cook for 8–10 min. Allow to stand for a few minutes.
2 Melt the butter for 1½ min, add the olive oil, parsley or sage and the garlic and heat for 1 min.
3 Add the drained beans, salt and pepper to taste, toss well, cover and cook for 3 min. Stir in the parmesan cheese to taste.
4 Serve hot garnished with chopped herbs.

Note: *A 225g (8oz) can of tomatoes may be added with the beans before stirring in the parmesan cheese. Allow an extra 1½ min cooking time.*

Barbecue baked beans (*serves 4*)

POWER LEVEL: 100% (FULL)

A quickly prepared variation of popular baked beans. This goes well with barbecued meats, hamburgers and sausages.

100g (4oz) streaky bacon rashers
2 medium tomatoes, skinned
25g (1oz) butter
1 onion, peeled and sliced
1 clove garlic, crushed
2 × 5ml tsp (2 tsp) brown sugar
½ × 5ml tsp (½ tsp) chilli powder
½ × 5ml tsp (½ tsp) mustard powder (dried mustard)
salt to taste
425g (15oz) can baked beans

1 Remove the rinds from the bacon rashers, place in a serving dish and cover with kitchen paper. Cook for 4–5 min until crispy. Remove the bacon rashers and drain on kitchen paper.
2 Chop the tomatoes roughly.
3 Melt the butter in the dish for 1 min in the microwave, add the onion and garlic.
4 Cover and cook for 4 min. Add the tomatoes, sugar, chilli powder, mustard powder, and salt to taste.
5 Stir well, cover and cook for 4–5 min. Add the baked beans, cover and cook for 3 min, stirring twice throughout.
6 Crumble the bacon over the top of the dish and serve hot.

Glazed onions (*serves 4–5*)

POWER LEVEL: 100% (FULL)

450g (1lb) button onions or shallots
boiling water
25g (1oz) butter
2 × 15ml tbsp (2 tbsp) caster sugar

1 Peel the onions and place in a large bowl or casserole dish. Pour on sufficient boiling water to cover.
2 Cover the dish and bring the water up to the boil in the microwave, drain leaving the onions in the dish.

3 Add the butter to the onions, cover and cook for 5 min. Shake the dish to stir the onions and sprinkle with the caster sugar.
4 Cook uncovered for 3–4 min until tender and glazed.
5 Serve hot.

Creamed mushrooms and peas (serves 4)
POWER LEVEL: 100% (FULL)
colour page 73

4 large rashers bacon
225g (8oz) button mushrooms, washed and sliced
350g (12oz) frozen peas
salt and freshly ground black pepper
pinch mixed herbs
150ml ($\frac{1}{4}$pt) double cream
For serving:
triangles of toasted or fried bread

1 Remove the rinds from the bacon and cut each rasher into strips.
2 Place the bacon strips into a serving dish, cover and cook for 2 min. Add the mushrooms, toss well in the fat from the bacon, cover and cook for 5–6 min.
3 Place the frozen peas in a bowl, cover and cook for 2½ min. Add salt, pepper and herbs, toss well, cover and cook for 2½–3½ min. Drain.
4 Add the peas to the mushrooms and bacon. Stir in the cream and adjust the seasoning.
5 Cook for 30–60 sec until just heated through without boiling.
6 Serve garnished with triangles of toasted or fried bread.

Asparagus flan (serves 6)
POWER LEVEL: 100% (FULL) AND 50% (DEFROST)
colour page 80

175g (6oz) light wholemeal pastry (page 32)
25g (1oz) butter or margarine
1 small onion, peeled and finely chopped
290g (10½oz) can condensed asparagus soup
3 eggs, beaten
3 × 15ml tbsp (3 tbsp) single cream or top of the milk
salt and pepper to taste
100g (4oz) cheese, grated
For decoration:
10–12 canned, frozen or fresh cooked asparagus spears

1 Roll out the pastry, line a 20cm (8in) flan dish and bake blind (page 32).
2 Melt the butter or margarine in a bowl for 1 min on 100% (full) setting, toss in the chopped onion and cook for a further 2–3 min until soft.
3 Beat together the soup, eggs, cream and seasoning until smooth and well blended. Stir in the cooked onion.
4 Cook the mixture on 50% (defrost) setting for 6–8 min until heated through, whisking every 2 min. Stir in the cheese.
5 Pour into the cooked flan case and cook on 50% (defrost) setting for 11–13 min, turning every 3 min. Allow to stand for a few minutes.
6 Heat the asparagus spears for 1–1½ min on 100% (full) setting and arrange on the top of the flan.
7 Serve on its own as a snack or with potatoes and salad as a main meal.

Pasta and rice

The main advantage of cooking pasta and rice by microwave is that the results are excellent, with pasta just right at the *al dente* stage and rice grains as they should be – separate, light and fluffy. In addition, little or no attention is required during the cooking period and the kitchen remains relatively free of steam. Cooking times are not much shorter but the great advantage is that reheating can be carried out most successfully; for best results, simply add a knob of butter to the pasta or rice or rinse under cold water before reheating.

Make sure the container is large enough to allow for the water to boil and the expansion of the pasta or rice during the cooking period when all dishes should be covered with a lid or clingfilm.

Defrosting and heating

To defrost 450g (1lb) of cooked pasta or rice, use a 50% (defrost) setting, cover the dish, and place in the microwave for 4–5 min. Stir gently halfway through, carefully breaking down the thawed food and removing from the dish if necessary. Any unthawed portion may be returned to the microwave for another minute or two. Alternatively, after the defrosting time, allow to stand for 2–3 min until completely thawed. Reheat on a 100% (full) setting for 3–4 min, again stirring halfway through; allow to stand for 1–2 min before serving.

Layered Noodle Pudding with Cheese Sauce (page 81) and Asparagus Flan (page 79)

Pasta and rice cooking chart

Pasta/Rice	Preparation	Cooking time 100% (Full)
egg noodles and tagliatelle 225g (8oz)	add 550ml (1pt) boiling salted water and 1 × 15ml tbsp (1 tbsp) oil	5–6 min stand 3 min
macaroni 225g (8oz)	add 550ml (1pt) boiling salted water and 1 × 15ml tbsp (1 tbsp) oil	8 min stand 3 min
pasta shells 225g (8oz)	add 850ml (1½pt) boiling salted water and 1 × 15ml tbsp (1 tbsp) oil	15–18 min stand 2 min
spaghetti 225g (8oz)	break spaghetti in half if necessary; add 850ml (1½pt) boiling salted water and 1 × 15ml tbsp (1 tbsp) oil	12 min stand 2 min
lasagne 225g (8oz)	add 1l (1¾pt) boiling salted water and 1 × 15ml tbsp (1 tbsp) oil	10 min stand 2 min
brown rice 225g (8oz)	add 550ml (1pt) boiling salted water	20–25 min stand 5 min
easy cook rice (American) 225g (8oz)	add 550ml (1pt) boiling salted water	12 min stand 5 min
long-grain rice (patna) 225g (8oz)	add 550ml (1pt) boiling salted water and 1 × 15ml tbsp (1 tbsp) oil	10 min stand 5 min

Layered noodle pudding (serves 4–6)

POWER LEVEL: 100% (FULL)
colour photograph opposite

This dish may be served as a substantial snack or with a meat dish as part of a main course.

225g (8oz) flat noodles eg tagliatelle
2 × 5ml tsp (2 tsp) oil
1 × 5ml tsp (1 tsp) salt
550ml (1pt) boiling water, approximately
75g (3oz) butter or margarine, melted
350g (12oz) cooked spinach, fresh or frozen
2 × 15ml tbsp (2 tbsp) single cream or top of the milk
salt and freshly ground black pepper
25g (1oz) parmesan cheese, grated
For serving:
275ml (½pt) cheese sauce (page 46)

1 Well butter a 850ml (1½pt) pudding basin.
2 Place the noodles in a bowl with the oil and salt and pour on sufficient boiling water to cover. Stir, cover and cook for 7–9 min until tender; stir twice.
3 Drain and rinse in hot running water. Drain well and stir in half the butter or margarine.
4 Mix well together the spinach, cream, seasonings, parmesan cheese and remaining butter or margarine.
5 Layer the buttered noodles and spinach mixture in the greased pudding basin, beginning and ending with a layer of noodles.
6 Cover with clingfilm, making a slit with the pointed end of a sharp knife. Cook for 5 min, turning every 2 min. Leave to stand for a few minutes.
7 Remove clingfilm, invert onto a hot serving plate or dish and serve with cheese sauce.

Spinach gratinée (serves 4)

POWER LEVEL: 100% (FULL)

225g (8oz) tagliatelle
25g (1oz) butter or margarine
1 small onion, peeled and finely chopped
450g (1lb) frozen spinach, thawed
150ml (¼pt) single cream
salt and freshly ground black pepper
100g (4oz) cheddar cheese, finely grated
25g (1oz) fresh white breadcrumbs
15g (½oz) butter
grated parmesan cheese for sprinkling, optional
grated nutmeg for sprinkling

1 Cook the tagliatelle in boiling, salted water (see adjoining chart) and drain well.
2 Melt 25g (1oz) butter in a large bowl for 1 min, add the onion, cover and cook for 2 min.
3 Add the spinach and heat through for 3 min. Stir in the cream and salt and pepper to taste.
4 Arrange layers of the tagliatelle, spinach and finely grated cheddar cheese in a serving dish.
5 Cover and heat through for 5–6 min. Scatter on the fresh white breadcrumbs, dot with the 15g (½oz) butter and sprinkle with the parmesan cheese if using.
6 Cook uncovered for 2–3 min until the butter is melted or, alternatively, brown under a hot grill.
7 Serve hot, sprinkled with grated nutmeg.

Scandinavian risotto (serves 4–6)
POWER LEVEL: 100% (FULL)

50g (2oz) butter
2 onions, chopped
1 stick celery, finely sliced
1 green pepper, deseeded and sliced
175g (6oz) long-grain rice
550ml (1pt) chicken stock
50g (2oz) raisins
salt and pepper
225g (8oz) cooked gammon
1 × 227g (8oz) can pineapple pieces

1 Melt the butter for 1 min in a large shallow dish. Add the vegetables and cook for 2 min. Add the rice and cook for a further 2 min or until the rice has absorbed the butter.
2 Pour in the stock and add the raisins and seasoning. Cover and cook for 15–20 min.
3 Cut the gammon into 6mm ($\frac{1}{4}$in) cubes, drain the pineapple and add both to the risotto. Stand for 10 min before serving.

Pasta salad (serves 6–8)
POWER LEVEL: 100% (FULL)

550ml (1pt) water
1 × 5ml tsp (1 tsp) salt
1 × 15ml tbsp (1 tbsp) oil
100g (4oz) shell pasta
50g (2oz) walnuts, chopped
50g (2oz) raisins
2 carrots
1 green eating apple
1 × 425g (15oz) can kidney beans
oil and vinegar salad dressing

1 Place water, salt and oil in a large bowl and heat in the cooker for 4 min. Add the pasta and cook for 10 min. Stir well, then drain and rinse with cold water.
2 Return the pasta to a serving bowl and stir in the walnuts and raisins.
3 Peel and dice the carrot; chop the apple, removing the core. Add carrot and apple to the salad.
4 Drain the kidney beans and rinse if necessary. Finally add the beans and the dressing to the salad and toss lightly before serving.

Kedgeree (serves 6–8)
POWER LEVEL: 100% (FULL)

Kedgeree is traditionally a breakfast dish but also makes a substantial supper dish.

500ml (18fl oz) boiling water
pinch salt
175g (6oz) long-grain rice
350g (12oz) smoked haddock
2 hard-boiled eggs
50g (2oz) butter
1 small onion, chopped
salt and pepper
1 × 15ml tbsp (1 tbsp) chopped parsley

1 Place the boiling water in a large casserole dish. Add the salt and stir in the rice. Cover and cook for 15 min. Leave to stand for 10 min when all the water should be absorbed; if not, drain the rice.
2 Wash and trim the fish, place in an ovenware dish, cover and cook for 4 min. Flake the fish, discarding the skin and the bones.
3 Chop one hard-boiled egg and slice the other. Melt the butter in a large dish for 2 min. Toss the onion in the butter. Cook for 4 min.
4 Add the rice, fish, chopped hard-boiled egg and seasoning. Mix well and warm through for 3–4 min.
5 Garnish with the sliced hard-boiled egg and chopped parsley before serving.

Mushroom-stuffed cannelloni (serves 4)
POWER LEVEL: 100% (FULL)

Serve as a main dish or as a starter course.

3 × 15ml tbsp (3 tbsp) oil
1 onion, peeled and finely chopped
2 cloves garlic, finely chopped
100g (4oz) mushrooms, chopped
1 × 5ml tsp (1 tsp) dried sweet basil
salt and freshly ground black pepper
4 tomatoes, skinned and chopped
8 cannelloni tubes
275ml ($\frac{1}{2}$pt) béchamel sauce (page 46)
25g (1oz) grated parmesan cheese
paprika pepper for sprinkling

1 Place 2 × 15ml tbsp (2 tbsp) of the oil in a large bowl, add the onions and garlic, toss well, cover and cook for $2\frac{1}{2}$ min.
2 Add the mushrooms, herbs and seasoning, cover and cook for 3 min. Stir in the tomatoes.
3 Cook the cannelloni in a large, covered bowl of boiling, salted water with the remaining 1 × 15ml tbsp (1 tbsp) oil for 5–6 min. Drain the pasta and rinse in cold water.
4 Fill the cannelloni with the mushroom mixture and place in a serving dish.
5 Heat the béchamel sauce, if necessary, and stir in half the cheese. Spoon the sauce over the cannelloni. Sprinkle with the rest of the cheese and paprika pepper.
6 Cook for 3–4 min until heated through and serve, handing more parmesan cheese separately.

Stuffed peppers (*serves 2*)

POWER LEVEL: 100% (FULL)
colour photograph above

2 medium green peppers
50g (2oz) long-grain rice
165ml (⅓pt) boiling chicken stock
1 onion, peeled and finely chopped
salt and pepper
1 bay leaf
50g (2oz) cooked ham or chicken, chopped
40g (1½oz) sultanas
For serving:
plain boiled rice

1 Cut a slice from the top of each pepper. Remove the core and seeds. Reserve the slice to use as a lid.
2 Cover and cook the peppers for 2 min, turn them over, cook for 2 min.
3 Place the rice in a bowl or dish, stir in the boiling chicken stock, onion, seasoning and bay leaf.
4 Cover and cook for 5 min, stir and cook for a further 3–5 min or until all the stock is absorbed. Remove the bay leaf.
5 Add the ham or chicken and sultanas to the rice. Fill the peppers with the rice mixture and replace the lids.
6 Stand the peppers in the serving dish, cover and cook for 3 min. Serve with a little extra boiled rice.

Stuffed Peppers (below) and German Red Cabbage (page 75)

Lasagne (*serves 6*)

POWER LEVEL: 100% (FULL) AND 70%

850ml (1½pt) approx bolognaise sauce, using 450g (1lb) minced beef (page 47)
425ml (¾pt) cheese sauce (page 46)
175g (6oz) lasagne
50g (2oz) cheese, grated
paprika pepper, for sprinkling

1 Make up and cook the bolognaise and cheese sauces. Cook the lasagne according to the chart on page 81.
2 When the lasagne is cooked, drain off the water and pat the leaves dry with kitchen paper towel.
3 Fill a large oblong or oval dish with alternate layers of cheese sauce, bolognaise sauce and lasagne, beginning and ending with cheese sauce.
4 Sprinkle with the grated cheese and paprika pepper. Cover and cook on 70% setting for 10–12 min, turning the dish once halfway through.
5 Serve hot.

Chicken pasta pie (serves 4–6)

POWER LEVEL: 100% (FULL) AND 50% (DEFROST)

225g (8oz) short-cut macaroni
2 × 5ml tsp (2 tsp) oil
1 × 5ml tsp (1 tsp) salt
550ml (1pt) boiling water, approximately
350g (12oz) cooked chicken, minced
100g (4oz) ham, minced
150ml (¼pt) top of the milk, or milk and single cream
2 × 5ml tsp (2 tsp) dried sage, thyme or basil
3 eggs, separated
1½ × 15ml tbsp (1½ tbsp) tomato purée
salt and freshly ground black pepper
For garnish:
50g (2oz) cheddar cheese, grated
1 × 15ml tbsp (1 tbsp) parmesan cheese

1 Well butter a 22.5cm (9in) round ovenware dish.
2 Place the macaroni in a bowl with the oil and salt and pour on sufficient boiling water to cover. Stir, cover and cook on 100% (full) setting for 8–10 min until plump and tender and most of the water has been absorbed. Stir twice.
3 Mix together the chicken, ham, milk, herbs, egg yolks, tomato purée and seasoning.
4 Whisk the egg whites until stiff and, with a metal spoon, fold into the meat mixture.
5 Rinse and drain the macaroni, place half in the bottom of the greased dish. Spread with the meat mixture and cover with the remaining macaroni.
6 Cover with clingfilm or a lid and cook on 50% setting for 15–18 min until cooked. Test the centre with a knife – the filling should be soft but set.
7 When cooked, leave to stand for 10–15 min. Garnish with the grated cheese and the parmesan cheese and serve hot.

Rice pilaf (serves 4)

POWER LEVEL: 100% (FULL)

Serve with meats, fish, casseroles or curries.

40g (1½oz) butter
1 small onion, chopped
225g (8oz) long-grain rice
425ml (¾pt) chicken stock
salt and pepper
75g (3oz) currants
75g (3oz) pistachio nuts or almonds, blanched and shredded

1 Melt the butter in a large shallow dish for 2 min. Add the onion and rice and cook for 3 min.
2 Add the stock and seasoning and cook, uncovered, for 12–15 min, adding extra stock if necessary.
3 Carefully stir in the currants and nuts before serving.

Aubergine macaroni pie (serves 4–6)

POWER LEVEL: 100% (FULL) AND 50% (DEFROST)

225g (8oz) aubergine, thinly sliced
salt
3 × 15ml tbsp (3 tbsp) olive oil, approximately
1 large onion, peeled and finely sliced
450g (1lb) minced beef
1–2 cloves garlic, crushed or finely chopped
salt and freshly ground black pepper
1 × 15ml tbsp (1 tbsp) tomato purée
400g (14oz) can tomatoes
1 × 5ml tsp (1 tsp) dried oregano or basil
275ml (½pt) natural yoghurt
2 eggs, beaten
100g (4oz) cheese, grated
225g (8oz) short-cut macaroni, cooked (see page 81)

1 Place the aubergine slices on a plate, sprinkle with salt and leave for 30 min. Rinse in cold water and dry.
2 Place in a large round casserole dish, sprinkle on the oil, cover and cook on 100% (full) setting for 4–5 min until soft. Remove the slices onto a plate.
3 Add the onion to the casserole dish with a little more oil if necessary and cook on 100% (full) setting for about 4 min until soft and transparent.
4 Add the minced beef, mix with the onion, cover and cook on 100% (full) setting for 5–6 min until browned, stirring once or twice and breaking down any lumps with a fork.
5 Add the garlic, seasoning, tomato purée, tomatoes and herbs. Cover and cook for a further 10–15 min until tender, stirring twice throughout.
6 Wipe the sides of the dish and arrange the aubergine slices on the meat.
7 Mix together the yoghurt, beaten eggs, three-quarters of the cheese and the cooked macaroni in a large bowl.
8 Cook on 50% setting for 4–5 min until hot. Pour the mixture over the aubergine slices.
9 Cook on 50% setting for 12–15 min until heated through and the topping is set.
10 Sprinkle with the remaining cheese and cook on 100% (full) setting for 1–2 min until melted or, alternatively, brown the top under a hot grill.

Fruits and puddings

Those favourite jam and syrup puddings that are almost a thing of the past because of the extent of the steaming period necessary, are available again with microwave cooking in just a fraction of the time. Jellies for trifles and gelatine for mousses can be melted in seconds and fresh fruit in wine or liqueur can be quickly prepared for a really delicious simple sweet. The range of desserts which may be prepared or cooked by microwave is almost never ending; the advantage being that they can be made in advance and served cold or reheated when required, in individual portions if necessary, according to your family's preference. Although traditional pies are not as successful because the fillings tend to boil out before the pastry tops are cooked, a selection of puddings, crumbles, flans and fruit dishes are all here ready for you to try.

When cooking steamed puddings in the microwave, they should be covered with clingfilm to keep in the moisture; however, they should be removed from the cooker while still slightly moist as cooking will continue and the puddings will set during the standing time.

Fresh fruit can be prepared in the normal way, sprinkled with sugar and cooked in a roasting bag or boiling bag in a similar manner to fresh vegetables. The fruit should be checked and stirred or turned regularly to make sure it does not overcook. When it is important that the fruit pieces do not break, cook them in a covered casserole when a little more liquid should be used and the cooking time increased accordingly to account for the extra volume in the oven. Fruits cooked in their skins, such as baked apples, should first be pricked or scored to prevent the fruits from bursting during the cooking process. As most fruits may be cooked with no additional liquid, they can soon be sieved or puréed to make sauces to pour over ice cream, natural yoghurt or puddings.

Fruit cooking chart

Fruit and quantity	Preparation	Cooking time 100% (full)	50% (defrost)
cooking apples 450g (1lb)	Peel, core and slice. Sprinkle with sugar to taste.	6–8 min	11–15 min
apricots 450g (1lb)	Stone and wash. Sprinkle with sugar to taste.	6–8 min	11–15 min
peaches 4 medium-sized	Stone and wash. Sprinkle with sugar to taste.	4–5 min	7–8 min
pears 6 medium-sized	Peel, halve and core. Dissolve 75g (3oz) sugar and a pinch of cinnamon in a little hot water. Pour over the pears.	8–10 min	15–20 min
plums, cherries, damsons, greengages 450g (1lb)	Stone and wash. Sprinkle with sugar to taste and add grated rind of $\frac{1}{2}$ lemon.	4–5 min	7–8 min
rhubarb 450g (1lb)	Trim, wash and cut into short lengths. Add 100g (4oz) sugar and grated rind of 1 lemon.	7–10 min	14–20 min
soft fruits 450g (1lb)	Top and tail currants, hull the berries. Wash well and add sugar to taste.	3–5 min	6–10 min

When thawing out a frozen dessert, it should be given short bursts of exposure to microwave energy, followed by a standing period. Repeat the process until the food is thawed and at an even temperature throughout.

Frozen fruits
Frozen fruits are partially defrosted by microwave and then allowed to stand at room temperature until completely thawed: see chart below.

Dried fruits
Although dried fruits can be cooked without soaking, it is preferable to soak them overnight in cold water before cooking, either conventionally or by micro-wave; this ensures plump and tender fruits. The exceptions are dates, figs, sultanas, raisins, etc, which do not require soaking before use in cake and pudding recipes unless specified.

After soaking 225g (8oz) dried fruits for 6–8 hours or overnight, drain them and place in a suitable microwave container. Add about 275ml ($\frac{1}{2}$pt) boiling water, grated lemon rind or juice, and sugar or syrup to taste and cook on 100% (full) setting for approximately 15 min, stirring or turning the dish once halfway through. Allow to stand for a few minutes before serving.

Fruit and quantity	50% (defrost)	100% (full)
in dry sugar 450g (1lb)	—	4–8 min
in sugar syrup 450g (1lb)	—	8–12 min
in dry pack (free flow or open frozen) 450g (1lb)	4–8 min	—

Apple bread pudding (cuts into 8 wedges)
POWER LEVEL: 100% (FULL) AND 50% (DEFROST)

225g (8oz) bread
225ml (8fl oz) milk
50g (2oz) butter or margarine
50g (2oz) demerara sugar
2 × 5ml tsp (2 tsp) mixed spice
1 egg, beaten
50g (2oz) mixed chopped peel
175g (6oz) mixed dried fruit (sultanas, raisins, currants, glacé cherries)
1 medium cooking apple
few drops lemon juice
demerara sugar for sprinkling

1 Lightly grease a 20cm (8in) flan dish.
2 Break the bread into small pieces and place in a bowl. Soak with milk, break down the bread with a fork. Beat thoroughly until smooth.
3 Melt the butter or margarine for 1$\frac{1}{2}$ min on 100% (full) setting; add to the bread with the sugar, spice, egg, peel and dried fruit. Mix together thoroughly.
4 Turn the mixture into the prepared dish and cook on 50% setting for 10 min. Leave to stand for 5 min.
5 Peel, core and slice the apple and arrange over the top of the pudding. Sprinkle the apple with a few drops of lemon juice.
6 Cook for a further 10 min on 50% setting.
7 Serve hot or cold sprinkled with demerara sugar.

Chocolate pudding (serves 6–8)
POWER LEVEL: 100% (FULL)

75g (3oz) plain chocolate
50g (2oz) butter or margarine
275ml ($\frac{1}{2}$pt) milk
75g (3oz) soft brown sugar
1 × 5ml tsp (1 tsp) vanilla essence
2 eggs, separated
150g (5oz) brown breadcrumbs
For serving:
chocolate sauce (page 44)

1 Lightly grease a 1$\frac{1}{4}$l (2pt) pudding basin.
2 Break up the chocolate and place in a bowl with the butter or margarine, milk, brown sugar and vanilla essence. Heat for about 2$\frac{1}{2}$ min then stir until blended.
3 Beat the egg yolks and stir into the chocolate mixture with the breadcrumbs.
4 Whisk the egg whites until stiff and fold into the mixture.
5 Pour into the prepared pudding basin and cover with clingfilm, slit with the pointed end of a sharp knife.
6 Cook for 6$\frac{1}{2}$–7$\frac{1}{2}$ min, turning once halfway through.
7 Leave to stand for 5 min before turning out.
8 Serve with a little chocolate sauce poured over the pudding and hand the rest of the sauce separately.

Cherry and praline flan (serves 6–8)

POWER LEVEL: 100% (FULL)
colour photograph below

1 × 20cm (8in) baked flan case using rich shortcrust
pastry (page 32)
1 × 15ml tbsp (1 tbsp) custard powder
2 × 5ml tsp (2 tsp) caster sugar
150ml ($\frac{1}{4}$pt) milk
150ml ($\frac{1}{4}$pt) double cream, whipped
100g (4oz) praline, crushed
2 × 450g (1lb) cans black cherries
2 × 5ml tsp (2 tsp) arrowroot
4 × 15ml tbsp (4 tbsp) redcurrant jelly
For serving:
whipped cream

1 Place the flan case on a large serving plate or in its
flan dish.
2 Make a custard with the custard powder, caster
sugar and milk, cook for 2–3 min, stirring every
minute until thick. Beat well then leave to cool.
3 When cold, whisk the custard and fold in the
whipped cream and praline. Place the mixture in
the bottom of the flan case and smooth the top.
4 Drain the cherries; reserve 150ml ($\frac{1}{4}$pt) of the juice
and blend this with the arrowroot.
5 Melt the redcurrant jelly for about 1 min and add to
the cherry juice and arrowroot. Stir well then heat

for 2–3 min until thick, stirring frequently.
6 Stone the cherries if necessary and arrange over the
praline cream. Glaze with the thickened juice and
leave to cool and set.
7 Serve cold with whipped cream.

Variation
Substitute finely chopped hazelnuts for the crushed
praline.

Note: *DO NOT FREEZE*

Praline

This is not really successful in the microwave so is best
made conventionally. Place equal weight quantities
of unblanched almonds and caster sugar into a
heavy-based saucepan and heat slowly over a low
heat until the sugar is melted and turned to a nut
brown colour. Stir with a metal spoon as soon as the
sugar starts to colour. Turn the mixture onto an oiled
tin or plate to cool. When cold, crush with a rolling
pin or grind it in a blender or liquidiser. Store in an
airtight container.

Cherry and Praline Flan (above)

Christmas pudding (serves about 12)
POWER LEVEL: 100% (FULL)
colour page 57

150g (5oz) plain flour
3 × 5ml tsp (3 tsp) mixed spice
175g (6oz) breadcrumbs
225g (8oz) soft brown sugar
225g (8oz) shredded suet
575g (1¼lb) mixed dried fruit (raisins, currants, sultanas)
50g (2oz) mixed chopped peel
50g (2oz) glacé cherries, quartered
1 orange, grated rind
1 medium dessert apple, peeled and grated
4 eggs
3 × 15ml tbsp (3 tbsp) black treacle
1 × 15ml tbsp (1 tbsp) malt extract
2 × 15ml tbsp (2 tbsp) milk
150ml (¼pt) stout
For serving:
cornflour sauce (page 48) and/or rum or brandy butter (page 47)

1 Lightly grease 3 × 550ml (1pt) pudding basins or 2 × 850ml (1½pt) pudding basins.
2 Sift the flour and spice into a large bowl. Add all the dry ingredients and mix well together.
3 Mix in all the other ingredients. (The mixture will improve in flavour if now left covered overnight in a cool place.)
4 Divide the mixture between the 3 smaller basins or the 2 larger ones. Cover each with clingfilm and make a slit in the top with the pointed end of a sharp knife.
5 Cook each small pudding for 5 min, or each larger one for 7–9 min. In either case, allow to stand for 5–10 min before turning out.
6 Serve hot with cornflour sauce and/or rum or brandy butter.

Note: *The puddings may be cooked and then left to mature wrapped in greaseproof paper and then in aluminium foil. On the day, they can be reheated in the microwave for 2–3 min, depending on size, or in individual portions for about 1 min each.*

Strawberry jelly mousse (serves 4–6)
POWER LEVEL: 100% (FULL)
colour page 27

1 × 298g (10oz) can strawberries
1 × 135g (4¾oz) strawberry jelly
1 small can evaporated milk, chilled

1 Drain the strawberries, reserving the juice. Break the jelly into squares and place in a 550ml (1pt) measuring jug.

2 Melt the jelly in the microwave for 30–45 sec and stir well.
3 Add the juice from the strawberries and make the jelly up to 550ml (1pt) with cold or chilled water. Mix well.
4 Pour the jelly into a large bowl and leave in the refrigerator until nearly set.
5 Whisk the jelly, gradually adding the evaporated milk in a thin stream. Whisk well together.
6 Stir in the strawberries and pour the mousse into clean moulds or a bowl and leave in the refrigerator until set.

Blackcurrant cobbler (serves 4–6)
POWER LEVEL: 100% (FULL)

Cobbler is a scone mix topping – delicious with blackcurrants but almost any stewed fruit can be used.

675g (1½lb) blackcurrants, fresh or frozen, thawed
75–100g (3–4oz) sugar
100g (4oz) self-raising flour
100g (4oz) wholemeal flour
pinch salt
½ × 5ml tsp (½ tsp) baking powder
50g (2oz) butter or margarine
25g (1oz) caster sugar
milk for mixing
demerara or soft brown sugar for sprinkling
For serving:
cream

1 Pick over and wash the fresh blackcurrants if used. Cover and cook the blackcurrants with the sugar for 4–5 min until just soft. Drain off some of the juice and reserve. Place the fruit in a 17.5–20cm (7–8in) dish.
2 Sift the self-raising flour, add the wholemeal flour, and stir in the salt and baking powder. Rub in the butter or margarine finely, stir in the caster sugar. Mix to a soft scone dough with the milk.
3 Knead lightly on a floured surface and roll out to 1.25cm (½in) thick. Cut into rounds with a 5cm (2in) cutter.
4 Arrange the scone rounds over the top of the fruit and brush with milk. Sprinkle with the sugar.
5 Cook for 5–6 min, turning twice throughout.
6 Serve hot or cold with cream and hand the reserved fruit juice separately.

Fruit crumble (serves 4)
POWER LEVEL: 100% (FULL)

675g (1½lb) fresh or canned fruit (use 900g (2lb) if the fruit has to be stoned)
100g (4oz) caster sugar
175g (6oz) plain flour
75g (3oz) butter

50g (2oz) demerara sugar
For serving:
custard sauce (page 48) or cream

1 Prepare the fruit, then place it in the bottom of a pie dish with the caster sugar.
2 Sift the flour into a bowl and rub in the butter. Stir in most of the demerara sugar.
3 Sprinkle the mixture over the fruit and top with the remaining demerara sugar.
4 Cook for 10–12 min, turning the dish halfway through the cooking time.

Apple and damson tansy (*serves 4*)
POWER LEVEL: 100% (FULL)
colour page 113

Tansy is a bitter-tasting herb which was once used for flavouring sweet dishes. The name now describes a pudding made from buttered fruit purée with eggs; the recipe dates back to the fifteenth century.

225g (8oz) cooking apples, peeled, cored and thinly sliced
225g (8oz) damsons, washed and stoned
50g (2oz) butter
100g (4oz) caster sugar
2 egg yolks
3 × 15ml tbsp (3 tbsp) fresh white breadcrumbs
150ml ($\frac{1}{4}$pt) double cream
2 × 5ml tsp (2 tsp) lemon juice
For serving:
whipped cream

1 Place the prepared fruit in a covered dish or a roasting bag with the butter.
2 Cook for 6–8 min or until the fruit is soft, stirring or shaking the fruit once halfway through.
3 Pass the fruit through a sieve or purée in a blender and then sieve. The purée should be fairly thick. If it is too thin, allow to boil in the microwave for a minute or two until reduced slightly.
4 Stir the sugar into the hot purée until dissolved. Beat in the egg yolks and breadcrumbs and leave until cold.
5 Whisk the cream lightly and fold into the mixture with the lemon juice to taste.
6 Place into individual serving glasses and chill in the refrigerator for an hour.
7 Serve piped with whipped cream.

DO NOT FREEZE

Oranges in caramel (*serves 4–6*)
POWER LEVEL: 100% (FULL)
colour page 95

8 oranges
225g (8oz) granulated sugar

150ml ($\frac{1}{4}$pt) cold water
1 × 5ml tsp (1 tsp) grand marnier, optional
150ml ($\frac{1}{4}$pt) warm water

1 Finely grate the rind of 3 of the oranges. Remove the peel and outer membrane from each fruit.
2 Hold the oranges over a serving dish. Slice the oranges, holding each one together with a wooden cocktail stick.
3 Stir the sugar into the cold water with the liqueur, if used. Bring to the boil in the microwave, without stirring, and cook until a light golden brown, approximately 10–12 min.
4 Quickly add the warm water to the caramel, protecting your hand from the steam with a towel. Return to the microwave for 30 sec. Stir well and leave to cool.
5 Pour the cooled caramel over the oranges in the serving dish and sprinkle with the grated orange rind. Chill well before serving.

Rice pudding (*serves 3–4*)
POWER LEVEL: 100% (FULL) AND 60%
colour page 57

50g (2oz) pudding rice
25g (1oz) caster sugar
25g (1oz) butter
550ml (1pt) milk
1 × 5ml tsp (1 tsp) ground nutmeg, optional
For decoration:
1 × 312g (11oz) can mandarin oranges, optional

1 Place all the ingredients except nutmeg in a $1\frac{1}{4}$l (2pt) dish or bowl and stir.
2 Leave the dish uncovered and bring to boiling point, 7–10 minutes on 100% (full) setting, stirring every 5 min.
3 Reduce to 60% setting and cook for 20–25 minutes stirring every 5 min.
4 Sprinkle with ground nutmeg or, when cold, decorate with mandarin oranges.

Chocolate semolina pudding (*serves 4*)
POWER LEVEL: 100% (FULL)

550ml (1pt) milk
40g ($1\frac{1}{2}$oz) semolina or ground rice
50g (2oz) caster sugar
15g ($\frac{1}{2}$oz) butter
50g (2oz) chocolate, broken into squares

1 Bring the milk to the boil in a $1\frac{1}{4}$l (2pt) pie dish. This will take approximately 5 min.
2 Add the semolina, sugar and butter; stir.
3 Cook for 5 min until thick, stirring frequently.
4 Add the chocolate and stir until melted.
5 Serve hot or cold.

Gooseberry fool (*serves 4–6*)
POWER LEVEL: 100% (FULL)

450g (1lb) gooseberries, topped and tailed
sugar to taste
1½ × 15ml tbsp (1½ tbsp) custard powder
1½ × 15ml tbsp (1½ tbsp) caster sugar
275ml (½pt) milk
few drops green colouring, optional
150ml (¼pt) double cream, whipped
For decoration:
2 × 15ml tbsp (2 tbsp) cream
few sprigs mint or angelica leaves

1 Wash the gooseberries and place in a roasting or boiling bag with sugar to taste.
2 Cook for 4–5 min until tender, shaking the bag once throughout. Leave to stand for a few minutes.
3 Mix the custard powder with the caster sugar. Blend in a little of the milk, then add the rest.
4 Cook uncovered for 3–4 min until bubbling and thick, stirring twice throughout.
5 Add to the gooseberries and put through a sieve, or purée in a blender. Add a few drops of green colouring, if necessary, to give a pale green tinge. Allow to cool slightly.
6 Stir in the double cream and pour·into a serving dish or individual glasses.
7 Stir in a little cream over the top to give a swirled effect.
8 Chill before serving, decorated with a few sprigs of mint or angelica leaves.

Sponge pudding (*serves 4*)
POWER LEVEL: 100% (FULL)
colour page 95

100g (4oz) butter
100g (4oz) caster sugar
2 eggs
100g (4oz) self-raising flour
few drops vanilla essence
For serving:
custard sauce (page 48)

1 Grease a 1¼l (2pt) pudding basin. Cream the butter and sugar in a mixing bowl, until light and fluffy.
2 Gradually beat in the eggs. Stir in the flour and vanilla essence then turn the mixture into the prepared basin.
3 Cook in the microwave for 5 min, or for 6 min if making one of the variations.

Variations
Syrup Place 3 × 15ml tbsp (3 tbsp) of golden syrup in the bottom of the basin. Add the pudding mixture and cook as above.
Sultana Stir 50–75g (2–3oz) of sultanas into the pudding mixture. Cook as above.

Jam Place 3 × 15ml tbsp (3 tbsp) of jam in the bottom of the basin. Add the pudding mixture and cook as above.
Pineapple Arrange 5 small pineapple rings in the prepared basin. Put a glacé cherry in the centre of each ring, then add the pudding mixture and cook as above.

Banana and apricot compôte (*serves 4–6*)
POWER LEVEL: 100% (FULL)

3 firm bananas
3 × 5 ml tsp (3 tsp) lemon juice
100g (4 oz) dried apricots, soaked overnight
25–50g (1–2oz) demerara sugar
50g (2oz) raisins
grated nutmeg for sprinkling
For serving:
whipped cream

1 Peel and slice the bananas and sprinkle with the lemon juice.
2 Place the apricots in a bowl with 150ml (¼pt) of the soaking liquid, add the sugar and raisins.
3 Cover and cook for 5 min until hot.
4 Pour the apricots and raisins over the bananas and allow to cool. Sprinkle with grated nutmeg.
5 Serve chilled with whipped cream.

DO NOT FREEZE

Crisp gooseberry pie (*serves 4–6*)
POWER LEVEL: 100% (FULL)

675g (1½lb) gooseberries
75–100g (3–4oz) sugar
25g (1oz) butter
½ × 5ml tsp (½ tsp) cinnamon
100g (4oz) plain flour
pinch salt
50g (2oz) rolled oats
75g (3oz) butter or margarine
100g (4oz) demerara sugar
For serving:
custard sauce (page 48)

1 Top and tail and wash the gooseberries,. Cover and cook them with the sugar, butter and cinnamon for 5–6 min until just soft. Drain off some of the juice and reserve. Place the fruit in a 20–22.5cm (8–9in) dish and leave to cool.
2 Sift the flour with the salt, stir in the rolled oats, and rub in the butter or margarine. Stir in the demerara sugar. This will make a coarse crumb mixture.
3 Sprinkle the mixture over the gooseberries and cook for 8–10 min until hot through and the topping is cooked. Turn 2 or 3 times throughout.
4 Serve hot or cold with custard sauce and hand the rest of the juice separately.

Pear and chocolate crumble (serves 4–6)

POWER LEVEL: 100% (FULL)
colour photograph below

675g (1½lb) dessert pears
sugar to taste
75g (3oz) plain flour
75g (3oz) wholemeal flour
pinch salt
75g (3oz) butter or margarine
50g (2oz) demerara sugar
50g (2oz) polka dots or chocolate chips
For serving:
chocolate sauce (page 44)

1 Lightly grease a 20–22.5cm (8–9in) round dish.
2 Peel, quarter and core the pears, and place in the base of the prepared dish. Sprinkle with sugar to taste.
3 Sift the plain flour, stir in the wholemeal flour and salt. Rub in the butter or margarine finely, stir in the demerara sugar and the polka dots or chocolate chips.
4 Sprinkle the mixture over the pears and cook for 10–12 min, giving a quarter turn every 3 min.
5 Serve with chocolate sauce.

Linzer torte (serves 6)

POWER LEVEL: 100% (FULL)
colour page 95

225g (8oz) almond pastry (page 92)
450g (1lb) raspberries, fresh or frozen, thawed
75–100g (3–4oz) caster sugar
2 × 15ml tbsp (2 tbsp) redcurrant jelly
For serving:
whipped cream

1 Prepare the almond pastry, roll out on a lightly floured surface and line a 20cm (8in) flan dish. Reserve the trimmings. Chill the flan case for about 20 min in the refrigerator.
2 Bake the flan case blind (page 32).
3 Fill the flan case with the raspberries and sugar. Roll out the reserved pastry, cut into strips and make a lattice design across the top of the flan.
4 Cook the flan for 7–8 min or until the lattice is cooked through. Allow to cool.
5 Warm the redcurrant jelly for 15–30 sec and brush over the lattice to make a thick glaze.
6 Serve cold with whipped cream.

Pear and Chocolate Crumble with Chocolate Sauce (above)

Almond pastry

225g (8oz) plain flour
pinch salt
pinch cinnamon
100g (4oz) butter
100g (4oz) caster sugar
1 lemon, grated rind
65g (2½oz) ground almonds
1 egg, beaten
1 egg yolk

1 Sift flour, salt and cinnamon together. Rub in the butter finely, stir in the sugar, lemon rind and ground almonds, mixing well together.
2 Beat the egg and egg yolk together and add to the dry ingredients. Mix well to form a soft dough.
3 Chill before rolling out.

Summer pudding (serves 6)
POWER LEVEL: 100% (FULL)
colour page 103

This pudding is 'uncooked' – packed full of blackcurrants, loganberries, raspberries and strawberries – and delicious when served with whipped cream.

675g (1½lb) blackcurrants, loganberries, raspberries, strawberries, mixed
100g (4oz) caster sugar
6–8 slices white bread, crusts removed
For serving:
whipped double cream

1 Pick over the fruits and wash. Place in a large bowl with the sugar, cover with a lid or clingfilm.
2 Cook for about 5 min, gently shaking or turning 2–3 times throughout to stir the contents without breaking the fruit. Leave to cool slightly, drain off and reserve some of the juice.
3 Line a 850ml (1½pt) pudding basin with the bread, starting by cutting to fit the base, then the sides. Cut the slices so that they fit closely together. Reserve some for the top.
4 Spoon the fruit into the basin and cover with the remaining bread. Place a plate that fits inside the basin over the pudding and press down with a weight.
5 Chill for about 8 hrs or overnight. Remove the weight and unmould the pudding onto a serving dish or plate.
6 Use the reserved juice to coat any parts of the bread which have not been soaked by the fruit juice during the chilling.
7 Serve with whipped cream.

Grapefruit in brandy (serves 4)
POWER LEVEL: 100% (FULL)

A refreshing sweet course after a rich meal.

3 large grapefruit, peeled
75g (3oz) demerara sugar
150ml (¼pt) water
1 × 5ml tsp (1 tsp) cinnamon
3 × 15ml tbsp (3 tbsp) brandy

1 Remove all the pith from the peeled grapefruit and carefully take out the core from the centre with a skewer. Cut the fruit into 1.25cm (½in) thick slices.
2 Add the sugar to the water with the cinnamon in a large, shallow dish.
3 Heat for 2 min, then stir until the sugar has dissolved in the water. Cook for a further 2 min, then lay the grapefruit slices in the syrup.
4 Cover and cook for 2–3 min, turning the slices over in the syrup halfway through.
5 Place the slices of grapefruit in a serving dish. Mix 3 × 15ml tbsp (3 tbsp) of the syrup with the brandy and pour over the fruit.
6 Serve hot or chilled on their own.

Honey baked apples (serves 4)
POWER LEVEL: 100% (FULL)
colour page 113

4 medium-sized cooking apples
40g (1½oz) butter
50g (2oz) soft brown sugar
25g (1oz) sultanas
2 × 15ml tbsp (2 tbsp) chopped walnuts
2 × 15ml tbsp (2 tbsp) water
1 × 15ml tbsp (1 tbsp) lemon juice
1½ × 15ml tbsp (1½ tbsp) clear honey
For serving:
cream

1 Core the apples but do not peel. Score them around the middle and place in a suitable serving dish.
2 Mix together the butter, sugar, sultanas and nuts. Fill the centre of each apple with the mixture.
3 Blend the water, lemon juice and honey together and spoon over the apples.
4 Cover the apples with lightly greased greaseproof paper and cook for 6–8 min.
5 Serve hot or cold with cream.

Note: *Cook 1 apple for 2–3 min; cook 2 apples for 4–5 min.*

Cakes, biscuits and scones

Home-made cakes can be cooked in the microwave most successfully, giving a good light texture. They do not brown as when baking in a conventional oven, but chocolate or coffee cakes or gingerbreads are 'self-coloured' anyway and there is much to be said for them being cooked so quickly. Prepared and frozen icing for decoration can be quickly thawed in the microwave and chocolate for a topping can be melted in 1–2 min, so it really is possible to bake a home-made cake or gateau in next to no time for that unexpected guest.

Any suitable container including paper may be used for cooking cakes, but straight-sided ones give good results and a better shape. The container may be lined with lightly greased greaseproof paper or with clingfilm but do not sprinkle with flour as this will only result in a doughy crust being formed on the outside of the finished cake. Make sure that the container is sufficiently large to allow for the mixture to rise; as a general guide, only half fill the dish with mixture. Generally, the wetter the mixture, the better the result. Cakes with a high proportion of fruit require lower settings for best results.

If during the cooking process, the mixture should appear to rise unevenly, it will normally level out towards the end of the cooking period; if in doubt, just turn the container approximately every 2 min. Overcooking causes dry, hard cakes, so remove from the oven when they seem slightly moist on top. As a general rule, when the cake has risen completely give it 1 min more cooking time then remove from the microwave. Although it is not usually necessary, should the outside of the cake be set before the centre, it is possible to protect these outside edges by covering with smooth pieces of aluminium foil for the last few minutes of the cooking period (see 'Aluminium Foil', page 9). After cooking, allow the cake to stand for 10–15 min before removing it on to a cooling tray.

Not all biscuit recipes are successful in the microwave; better results are from those mixtures which are cut into pieces after cooking. However, the few recipes included in this section are well worth trying and good results can be obtained.

I have included some scone recipes as they are very quickly cooked and can almost be made while the rest of the tea is being prepared.

Defrosting

When thawing a large, frozen, cream cake, give it only $\frac{1}{2}$–$\frac{3}{4}$ min exposure to microwave energy and then let it stand until completely thawed, otherwise the cream may melt before the cake is completely thawed; it is better to allow individual cream cakes to thaw naturally. Other large cakes may be given 2–3 minutes in the microwave and then allowed to stand for 5–10 minutes before serving. An individual cake, scone or slice of cake requires only 15–30 sec in the microwave depending on size and type and is then allowed to stand for 2 min before serving. Do not allow frozen cakes to get hot when thawing as this may result in a dry cake. As soon as it feels warm, remove the cake from the cooker and allow it to stand and heat equalise. If it is not then completely thawed, put it back into the microwave for another minute.

Most biscuits will thaw out very quickly at room temperature; one or two should be heated in the microwave for no longer than 10–25 sec and a plate of biscuits for no longer than 1 min. Leave them to stand for a few minutes before serving.

'One stage' victoria sandwich (cuts into 8)
POWER LEVEL: 100% (FULL)

175g (6oz) soft margarine
175g (6oz) caster sugar
3 eggs, beaten
175g (6oz) self-raising flour
pinch salt
2 × 15ml tbsp (2 tbsp) hot water
jam, or buttercream
icing sugar for dusting

1 Line a 18.75–20cm (7$\frac{1}{2}$–8in) cake dish with clingfilm or lightly grease and line the base with greaseproof paper.
2 Place all the ingredients except the jam and icing sugar into a bowl and mix until combined, then beat well until smooth.
3 Place the mixture into the prepared dish, smooth the top and cook for 6$\frac{1}{2}$–7$\frac{1}{2}$ min. Leave for 5–10 min before placing on a cooling rack.
4 When cold, cut in half horizontally and sandwich together with jam or buttercream. Dust the top with icing sugar.

Whisked sponge (cuts into 8)
POWER LEVEL: 100% (FULL)

A light sponge cake which relies on the whisking of air into the eggs as the raising agent, best eaten on the day it is made.

4 eggs
100g (4oz) caster sugar

100g (4oz) plain flour
pinch salt
jam
whipped cream
icing sugar for dusting

1 Line a 18.75–20cm (7$\frac{1}{2}$–8in) cake dish with clingfilm, or lightly grease and line the base with greaseproof paper.
2 Whisk the eggs and sugar together until trebled in volume and really thick and creamy.
3 Sift the flour and salt and sprinkle over the mixture, very carefully folding in with a metal spoon and turning the mixture over from the base of the bowl to ensure that all the flour is mixed in.
4 Pour into the prepared container and cook for 4$\frac{1}{2}$–5 min. Leave for 5–10 min before placing on a cooling rack.
5 When cold, cut in half horizontally and sandwich the two halves together with jam and cream. Dust the top with icing sugar.

Genoese sponge sandwich (cuts into 8)
colour photograph opposite

This cake has better keeping qualities than the whisked sponge and makes a good base for various fillings and toppings for richer gâteaux.

Follow the ingredients and method for the previous recipe. Melt 50g (2oz) butter for 1–1$\frac{1}{2}$ min and add to the thickened mixture with the flour by pouring the melted butter in a thin stream down the side of the bowl whilst folding in the flour and butter with a metal spoon. Fold in very carefully, ensuring that the spoon cuts across the base of the bowl so that all the flour and butter are well mixed in. Cook and decorate as for the whisked sponge, or fill and coat with buttercream and decorate with toasted almonds or fruit.

Buttercream
Soften 75g (3oz) butter and gradually add 175g (6oz) sifted icing sugar. Beat well after each addition and then beat until light and fluffy. Flavour and colour as required.

Oranges in Caramel (page 89), Sponge Pudding (page 90) and Linzer Torte (page 91)

Peanut Butter Cookies (page 98), Shortbread (page 98), Genoese Sponge (above) and Sultana Cake (page 100)

Queen cakes (*makes about 24*)
POWER LEVEL: 100% (FULL)

175g (6oz) butter or margarine
175g (6oz) caster sugar
3 eggs
175g (6oz) self-raising flour
pinch salt
75g (3oz) currants
milk for mixing
24 paper cases, approximately

1 Place 6 paper cake cases into a 6-ring microwave muffin pan, or individual small dishes or cups.
2 Cream the butter or margarine, add the sugar and beat well together until light and fluffy.
3 Add the eggs gradually, beating well after each addition.
4 Sift the flour and salt and toss in the currants. Fold into the creamed mixture with a metal spoon.
5 Mix in sufficient milk to give a soft dropping consistency.
6 Place spoonfuls of the mixture into the paper cases until no more than two-thirds full.
7 Cook for 2–2½ min, turning or rearranging once halfway through.
8 Remove onto a cooling rack and cook the remainder in batches of 6.

Variations
Omit the currants and replace with one of the following:
75g (3 oz) finely chopped dates
75g (3oz) finely chopped glacé cherries
75g (3oz) polka dots (chocolate chips)
75g (3oz) finely chopped crystallised ginger
75g (3oz) chopped walnuts
75g (3oz) sultanas

Sticky gingerbread (*cuts into 12–16 wedges*)
POWER LEVEL: 100% (FULL) AND 75%

100g (4oz) butter or margarine
225g (8oz) black treacle
75g (3oz) soft brown sugar
2 × 15ml tbsp (2 tbsp) orange marmalade
150ml (¼pt) milk
½ × 5ml tsp (½ tsp) bicarbonate of soda
100g (4oz) self-raising flour
2 × 5 ml tsp (2 tsp) ground ginger
1 × 5ml tsp (1 tsp) mixed spice
100g (4oz) wholemeal flour
2 eggs, beaten
apricot glaze (page 114)

1 Line a 22.5cm (9in) cake dish with clingfilm.
2 Place the butter or margarine, treacle, sugar and orange marmalade into a bowl, heat on 100% (full) setting for 2–3 min then stir until blended.
3 Warm the milk for 30 sec on 100% (full) setting and stir in the bicarbonate of soda.
4 Sift the self-raising flour and spices, stir in the wholemeal flour.
5 Add the treacle mixture, milk and eggs to the dry ingredients and mix thoroughly until smooth.
6 Pour the mixture into the prepared dish and cook on 75% setting for 12–14 min, turning every 3 min.
7 Place on a cooling rack and, when cool, brush with apricot glaze. Serve cut into wedges.

Fruit gingerbread
colour page 99

Follow the ingredients and method for sticky gingerbread, adding 50g (2oz) sultanas or raisins or chopped crystallised ginger or pineapple to the dry ingredients. When cool, brush with apricot glaze and decorate with flaked almonds.

Note: *If your microwave cooker has no variable power control setting, either divide the above mixture into two and cook each separately, or make up half quantity. Place in a 15cm (6in) cake dish and cook for 3½–4½ min at 100% (full) setting.*

Rum truffle cakes (*makes about 12*)
POWER LEVEL: 100% (FULL)

These are delicious and are quick and easy to make; the mixture is quite rich so smaller ones could be made for petits fours to serve with coffee after a meal.

50g (2oz) butter
100g (4oz) plain chocolate
275g (10oz) cake crumbs, approximately
75g (3oz) icing sugar, sifted
75g (3oz) seeded raisins, finely chopped
75g (3oz) glacé cherries, finely chopped
3 × 15ml tbsp (3 tbsp) apricot jam, sieved
2 × 15ml tbsp (2 tbsp) rum, or
2 × 5ml tsp (2 tsp) rum essence
chocolate vermicelli or
desiccated coconut for coating.

1 Melt the butter and chocolate for 1½–2 min. Stir until well blended.
2 Add all the remaining ingredients except the vermicelli or coconut, and mix well together. If the mixture is too dry, add a little more jam or rum. If it is too wet, add a few more cake crumbs.
3 Allow the mixture to cool before forming into balls and rolling in the chocolate vermicelli or desiccated coconut.
4 Place in decorative paper cake cases before serving.

Rich fruit cake (*cuts into 8 or 12*)
POWER LEVEL: 40%
colour page 31

Although it is difficult to obtain good results with rich fruit cake mixtures, this recipe has been developed especially for the microwave using a low power setting.

2 eggs, beaten
2 × 15ml tbsp (2 tbsp) black treacle
175g (6oz) dark soft brown sugar
2½ × 15ml tbsp (2½ tbsp) oil
175g (6oz) self-raising flour
½ × 5ml tsp (½ tsp) salt
1 × 5ml tsp (1 tsp) mixed spice
150ml (¼pt) milk
450g (1lb) mixed dried fruit
50g (2oz) glacé cherries, quartered
50g (2oz) mixed chopped peel
50g (2oz) chopped nuts

1 Lightly grease a 18.75cm (7½in) round cake dish and line the base with a circle of greaseproof paper.
2 Mix together the eggs, treacle, sugar and oil. Sift the flour, salt and mixed spice.
3 Gradually stir in the flour mixture alternately with the milk. Mix thoroughly.
4 Add the fruit, peel and nuts and place the mixture into the prepared container; smooth the top.
5 Cook on 40% setting for 40–50 min or until a skewer leaves the centre of the cake clean.
6 Leave for 30–40 min before turning out onto a cooling rack.

Note: *The cake may be decorated with marzipan and glacé fruits or royal icing, in which case it is best left to mature for up to a week well wrapped in greaseproof paper and aluminium foil.*

Chocolate cup cakes (*makes 12–16*)
POWER LEVEL: 100% (FULL)

75g (3oz) self-raising flour
25g (1oz) cocoa
pinch salt
50g (2oz) butter or margarine
50g (2oz) soft brown sugar
1 egg, beaten
120ml (4fl oz) milk, approximately
chocolate fudge icing (page 100) or melted chocolate
hazelnuts, optional
16 paper cases, approximately

1 Place 6 paper cases into a 6-ring microwave muffin pan, or individual small dishes or cups.
2 Sift the flour, cocoa and salt into a bowl. Rub in the butter or margarine finely, stir in the sugar.
3 Mix in the egg and the milk to form a very soft, almost runny mixture.

4 Half fill the paper cases with the mixture and cook for 2 min, turning or rearranging after 1 min.
5 Remove the cakes onto a cooling rack and cook the remainder in batches of 6 and 4.
6 When cold, coat the top of each cake with chocolate fudge icing or melted chocolate. Decorate with a hazelnut on the top of each cake.

DO NOT ICE BEFORE FREEZING. DECORATE JUST BEFORE SERVING

Double deckers (*makes 6*)
POWER LEVEL: 100% (FULL)
colour page 27

6 squares chocolate
12 digestive biscuits
6 marshmallows

1 Place the 6 squares of chocolate on top of 6 of the biscuits. Arrange in a circle on a plate or on the microwave shelf.
2 Cook for 2–2½ min, remove from the oven and spread the chocolate over the biscuits with a knife.
3 Place the 6 marshmallows on top of the remaining 6 biscuits and arrange in the microwave. Cook for ¾–1¼ min until the marshmallows have 'puffed up'.
4 To make the double deckers, put a chocolate-covered biscuit on top of each melted marshmallow. Leave to cool slightly before serving.

DO NOT FREEZE

Flapjacks (*cuts into 8 wedges*)
POWER LEVEL: 100% (FULL)

3 × 15ml tbsp (3 tbsp) golden syrup
100g (4oz) demerara sugar
100g (4oz) butter or margarine
225g (8oz) rolled oats
1 × 5ml tsp (1 tsp) baking powder
½ × 5ml tsp (½ tsp) salt
1 egg, beaten

1 Line a 20cm (8in) round dish with clingfilm.
2 Place the syrup, sugar and butter into a bowl and heat for 2–2½ min. Stir until well blended and the sugar is dissolved.
3 Stir in the remaining ingredients and place in the prepared container.
4 Cook for 4–5 min, turning every 1¼ min.
5 Leave for a few minutes to set and then mark into wedges.
6 When cool, remove from the dish and serve cut into wedges.

Rich sultana and cherry cake (*cuts into 8*)
POWER LEVEL: 60%

175g (6oz) glacé cherries
350g (12oz) sultanas
100g (4oz) plain flour
pinch salt
75g (3 oz) butter
1 lemon, grated rind
75g (3oz) caster sugar
2 eggs, beaten

1 Lightly grease an 18.75cm (7½in) round cake dish and line the base with a circle of greaseproof paper.
2 Wash and dry the cherries thoroughly. Cut in half and mix with the sultanas.
3 Sift the flour with the salt and add about a third to the cherries and sultanas. Toss so that the fruit is lightly coated with the flour.
4 Cream the butter, add the lemon rind and sugar and beat together until light and fluffy.
5 Add the eggs gradually, beating well after each addition.
6 Fold in the flour alternately with the fruit.
7 Place into the prepared container and smooth the top.
8 Cook for 12–15 min turning every 3 min, or until a skewer leaves the centre of the cake clean.
9 Leave for 20–30 min before turning out onto a cooling rack.

Cherry and walnut ring cake
(*cuts into 8–10*)
POWER LEVEL: 100% (FULL)

100g (4oz) butter or margarine
100g (4oz) caster sugar
2 eggs, beaten
175g (6oz) self-raising flour
pinch salt
50g (2oz) walnuts, chopped
1–2 × 15ml tbsp (1–2 tbsp) milk
100g (4oz) glacé cherries, halved
icing sugar for dusting

1 Lightly grease a 20cm (8in) microwave ring mould and line base with greaseproof paper or line with clingfilm.
2 Cream the butter or margarine until soft, add the sugar and beat well until light and fluffy.
3 Add the eggs gradually, beating well after each addition.
4 Sift the flour and salt and fold into the creamed mixture with a metal spoon. Add the walnuts and milk, mix well to form a soft mixture.
5 Place the cherries over the base of the container and spoon in the mixture.
6 Cook for 5–6 min, turning once halfway through if

necessary. Leave for 10–15 min before turning onto a cooling tray.
7 When cool, dust heavily with icing sugar.

Cherry and coconut ring cake
colour photograph opposite

Follow the ingredients and method for cherry and walnut ring cake, substituting 50g (2oz) desiccated coconut for the walnuts. More milk will be necessary to make a soft mixture. Decorate with toasted coconut.

Toasted desiccated coconut
POWER LEVEL: 100% (FULL)

Place the coconut onto a flat dish or plate or in a roasting bag and cook in the microwave, stirring or shaking frequently, for about 5 min or until the required toasted colour has been obtained.

Peanut butter cookies (*makes about 36*)
POWER LEVEL: 100% (FULL)
colour page 95

100g (4oz) butter
225g (8oz) soft brown sugar
100g (4oz) peanut butter
1 egg, beaten
175g (6oz) plain flour
¼ × 5ml tsp (¼ tsp) baking powder
¼ × 5ml tsp (¼ tsp) salt
1 × 5ml tsp (1 tsp) vanilla essence

1 Cream the butter, add the sugar and beat well until soft. Beat in the peanut butter and the egg.
2 Sift the flour, baking powder and salt. Fold into the creamed mixture and add the vanilla essence.
3 Form the mixture into small balls, allowing 2 × 5ml tsp (2 tsp) mixture for each. Flatten the balls of dough with a fork dipped in sugar.
4 Place 6 at a time on a microwave baking tray or on lightly greased greaseproof paper on the cooker shelf and cook for 1¾–2½ min depending on size. Turn once halfway through.
5 Leave to cool on a wire rack.

Shortbread (*makes 8 wedges*)
POWER LEVEL: 100% (FULL)
colour page 95

75g (3oz) plain flour
75g (3oz) wholemeal flour
50g (2oz) ground rice
pinch salt
150g (5oz) butter
25g (1oz) caster sugar
caster sugar for dusting

1 Line a 17.5cm (7in) flan dish with clingfilm.
2 Sift the flours, rice and salt into a mixing bowl.
3 Rub in the butter finely.
4 Stir in the sugar and bring the mixture together with the palm of the hand and knead lightly.
5 Press the mixture into the prepared dish and smooth the top with a palette knife.
6 Mark into 8 and prick well with a fork.
7 Cook for 3–4 min, giving a quarter turn every minute.
8 Cool slightly, sprinkle with sugar then cut into pieces. Turn out and leave to cool on a cooling rack.

Caramel shortbread *(makes 8 wedges)*
POWER LEVEL: 100% (FULL)

Shortbread mixture (as above)

For the topping:
50g (2oz) butter
50g (2oz) caster sugar
1 × 15ml tbsp (1 tbsp) golden syrup
200g (7oz) condensed milk
75g (3oz) plain chocolate

Cherry and Coconut Ring Cake (page 98), Fruit Gingerbread (page 96) and Coconut Cake (page 100)

1 Follow the ingredients and method for shortbread using all plain flour. When cooked, leave in the dish and prepare the topping.
2 Place all the ingredients except the chocolate into a bowl and heat for about 3 min. Stir until well blended and the sugar is dissolved.
3 Heat until boiling and, stirring every $\frac{1}{2}$ min, boil until thickened.
4 Leave to cool for 1 min before pouring over the shortbread base. Leave to cool and set.
5 Melt the chocolate for 2–2$\frac{1}{2}$ min and spread over the topping.
6 Mark into serving portions and leave until quite cold before cutting into wedges and removing from the dish.

Note: *The wholemeal flour gives a nutty texture to the shortbread but, if preferred use all plain white flour.*

Basic cake mixture (cuts into 8)
POWER LEVEL: 100% (FULL)

225g (8oz) self-raising flour
pinch salt
100g (4oz) butter or margarine
100g (4oz) soft brown sugar
2 eggs, beaten
few drops lemon juice
milk for mixing
apricot glaze, optional (page 114)

1 Line a 18.75–20cm (7½–8in) cake dish with clingfilm or lightly grease and line the base with greaseproof paper.
2 Sift the flour and the salt, rub in the butter or margarine finely, stir in the sugar.
3 Mix in the eggs, lemon juice and sufficient milk to form a soft dropping consistency.
4 Turn the mixture into the prepared dish and cook for 5½–7 min. Allow to cool slightly before removing from the dish onto a cooling rack.
5 When cold, brush with apricot glaze.

Fruit cake

Follow the ingredients and method for the basic cake mixture adding 150g (5oz) mixed dried fruit to the dry ingredients after the sugar.

Sultana cake
colour page 95

Follow the ingredients and method for the basic cake mixture, adding 150g (5oz) sultanas to the dry ingredients after the sugar.

Coconut cake
colour page 99

Follow the ingredients and method for the basic cake mixture, adding 175g (6oz) desiccated coconut to the dry ingredients after the sugar; a little more milk for mixing may be required. When cold, decorate with glacé icing (see below) and toasted coconut (page 98).

Glacé icing

Mix 175g (6oz) sifted icing sugar with sufficient hot water to make a soft paste, thick enough to coat the back of the spoon. Mix well and use immediately.

DO NOT ICE BEFORE FREEZING. DECORATE JUST BEFORE SERVING

Chocolate honey cake (cuts into 8)
POWER LEVEL: 100% (FULL)

175g (6oz) butter
75g (3oz) demerara sugar
2 × 15ml tbsp (2 tbsp) clear honey
3 eggs, beaten
125g (4½oz) self-raising flour
40g (1½oz) cocoa
1 × 5ml tsp (1 tsp) instant coffee
4 × 15ml tbsp (4 tbsp) hot water
few drops vanilla essence
chocolate fudge icing (see below)

1 Lightly grease an 18.75cm (7½in) cake dish and line the base with a circle of greaseproof paper.
2 Cream the butter, add the sugar and honey and beat well together until light and fluffy.
3 Add the eggs gradually, beating well after each addition.
4 Sift the flour and cocoa together and fold into the creamed mixture with a metal spoon.
5 Dissolve the coffee in the hot water and fold into the mixture with the vanilla essence.
6 Place mixture into the prepared container and cook for 5½–6½ min.
7 Leave until cool before turning out onto a wire rack.
8 When cold, cut in half horizontally. Sandwich the two halves together with half the fudge icing and pour the remainder over the top.

Chocolate fudge icing
POWER LEVEL: 100% (FULL)

25g (1oz) butter
50g (2oz) soft brown or demerara sugar
2 × 15ml tbsp (2 tbsp) cocoa
3 × 15ml tbsp (3 tbsp) cold water
2 × 5 ml tsp (2 tsp) milk
225g (8oz) icing sugar, sifted
2 × 15ml tbsp (2 tbsp) warm water
few drops vanilla essence

1 Place the butter and sugar into a large bowl. Blend the cocoa with the cold water and add to the bowl with the milk.
2 Heat for 1–2 min, stir until the sugar is dissolved.
3 Heat until boiling, then allow to boil for 2–2½ min.
4 Add icing sugar, warm water and vanilla essence. Mix well together then beat well for 5 min.
5 Pour over the cake whilst still warm as this icing sets when cold.

Toffee mallow crunch (makes about 20–25)
POWER LEVEL: 100% (FULL)
colour page 27

100g (4oz) soft toffees
100g (4oz) butter
100g (4oz) marshmallows
150g (5oz) Rice Krispies

1 Unwrap the toffees and put them into a large mixing bowl with the butter. Cover and cook for 3 min.
2 Stir the toffee mixture and add the marshmallows. Cover and heat for another 2 min, then stir again.
3 Add half the Rice Krispies to the mixture and stir well, making sure all the Krispies are covered with toffee. Add the rest of the Krispies and stir well again.
4 Press the mixture into greased square or oblong tins or dishes and leave to cool before cutting into squares. Alternatively, make small rock shapes from spoonfuls of the mixture on trays and leave to cool and set.

DO NOT FREEZE

Almond slices (*makes about 12 slices*)
POWER LEVEL: 75%

3 egg whites
100g (4oz) ground almonds
175g (6oz) caster sugar
50g (2oz) self-raising flour
few drops almond essence
25–50g (1–2oz) almonds, blanched and chopped

1 Lightly grease a dish approximately 15 × 15cm (6 × 6in) square or an equivalent-size oblong dish.
2 Whisk the egg whites until stiff and holding shape, then using a metal spoon carefully fold in the ground almonds, caster sugar, sifted flour and almond essence.
3 Place the mixture into the prepared dish, smooth the top and scatter with the chopped almonds.
4 Cook on 75% setting for 5–6 min, turning every $1\frac{1}{2}$ min.
5 Leave to cool for a few minutes before cutting into slices and removing to a wire rack to cool.

Walnut and chocolate brownies
(*makes 12–16*)
POWER LEVEL: 100% (FULL)

50g (2oz) butter or margarine
50g (2oz) plain chocolate
150g (5oz) dark soft brown sugar
50g (2oz) self-raising flour
pinch salt
2 eggs, beaten
$\frac{1}{2}$ × 5ml tsp ($\frac{1}{2}$ tsp) vanilla essence
50g (2oz) walnuts, chopped
demerara sugar for sprinkling

1 Line a 17.5cm (7in) square dish or an equivalent-size oblong dish.
2 Melt the butter and chocolate for about 3 min, mix well together and add the sugar.
3 Sift the flour and salt into a bowl and add the chocolate mixture, eggs, vanilla essence and walnuts. Beat until smooth and pour into the prepared container.
4 Cook for 4–5 min, turning every minute.
5 Leave for 1–2 min to cool slightly before sprinkling with demerara sugar.
6 Mark into squares and leave to cool before cutting and serving.

101

Cheesy scone round (cuts into 6 or 8 wedges)
POWER LEVEL: 100% (FULL)

175g (6oz) self-raising flour
$\frac{1}{2}$ × 5ml tsp ($\frac{1}{2}$ tsp) salt
$\frac{1}{2}$ × 5ml tsp ($\frac{1}{2}$ tsp) baking powder
pinch pepper
$\frac{1}{4}$ × 5ml tsp ($\frac{1}{4}$ tsp) dry mustard
40g (1$\frac{1}{2}$oz) butter or margarine
50g (2oz) cheese, finely grated
milk for mixing
paprika pepper

1 Lightly grease a 17.5cm (7in) round flan dish and line the base with greaseproof paper.
2 Sift the flour, salt, baking powder and seasonings into a bowl, rub in the butter or margarine finely.
3 Reserve 1 × 15ml tbsp (1 tbsp) of the cheese. Stir the remainder into the flour with sufficient milk to mix to a soft manageable dough. Knead lightly on a floured surface.
4 Roll out into a round approximately 17.5cm (7in) diameter. Place into the prepared container. Score to half the depth into 6 or 8 wedges.
5 Cook for approximately 5 min, turning the dish once halfway through.
6 When cooked, sprinkle with the reserved grated cheese mixed with paprika pepper to taste.
7 Split into wedges and serve hot or cold with butter.

Spicy scone round (cuts into 6)
POWER LEVEL: 100% (FULL)

175g (6oz) self-raising flour
pinch salt
1 × 5ml tsp (1 tsp) mixed spice
$\frac{1}{2}$ × 5ml tsp ($\frac{1}{2}$ tsp) baking powder
40g (1$\frac{1}{2}$oz) butter or margarine
2 × 5ml tsp (2 tsp) sugar
milk for mixing

1 Lightly grease a 17.5cm (7in) round flan dish and line the base with greaseproof paper.
2 Sift the flour, salt, mixed spice and baking powder, rub in the butter or margarine finely.
3 Stir in the sugar and sufficient milk to make a soft manageable dough. Knead lightly on a floured surface.
4 Roll out to about 1.25cm ($\frac{1}{2}$in) thick. Using a 6.25cm (2$\frac{1}{2}$in) cutter, cut into 6 rounds.
5 Place 5 shapes round the outside edge of the container and 1 in the centre.
6 Cook for 2 min, turn, cook for 1–2 min.
7 Serve hot or cold, split and spread with butter.

Iced scone round

Follow the ingredients and method for spicy scone round. When cooked and cool, decorate the top of the scone round with glacé icing (page 100), quartered glacé cherries and a sprinkling of chopped almonds or walnuts.

DO NOT FREEZE WHEN ICED AND DECORATED

Singin' hinnie (cuts into 6)
POWER LEVEL: 100% (FULL)

This is a girdle cake from Northumberland, so called because it traditionally sizzles ('sings') as it cooks. In the microwave, it is cooked in a browning dish.

100g (4oz) plain flour
$\frac{1}{4}$ × 5ml tsp ($\frac{1}{4}$ tsp) bicarbonate of soda
$\frac{1}{4}$ × 5ml tsp ($\frac{1}{4}$ tsp) cream of tartar
$\frac{1}{4}$ × 5ml tsp ($\frac{1}{4}$ tsp) salt
25g (1oz) lard or butter
25g (1oz) sugar
40g (1$\frac{1}{2}$oz) currants
1 egg, beaten
milk for mixing
oil

1 Sift the flour, raising agents and salt into a bowl. Rub in the lard or butter finely, add the sugar and currants. Mix well together.
2 Add the egg and sufficient milk to give a soft manageable dough.
3 Knead on a floured surface and roll or shape into a round, about 1.25cm ($\frac{1}{2}$in) thick.
4 Preheat the browning dish for 3$\frac{1}{2}$–4 min, depending on size, and lightly brush the base with oil.
5 Quickly place the cake into the browning dish, cook for 1$\frac{1}{2}$–2 min, turn the cake over and the dish around, cook for 1–1$\frac{1}{2}$ min.
6 Cool, split in half horizontally, butter and sandwich together again. Serve while still warm.

Wholemeal scones (cuts into 6 or 8 wedges)
POWER LEVEL: 100% (FULL)

100g (4oz) plain flour
pinch salt
1 × 5ml tsp (1 tsp) bicarbonate of soda
1 × 5ml tsp (1 tsp) cream of tartar
100g (4oz) wholemeal flour
2 × 5ml tsp (2 tsp) sugar
50g (2oz) butter or margarine
150ml ($\frac{1}{4}$pt) buttermilk or fresh milk with 1$\frac{1}{2}$ × 5ml tsp (1$\frac{1}{2}$ tsp) baking powder

1 Lightly grease a 17.5cm (7in) round flan dish and line the base with greaseproof paper.
2 Sift the flour, salt, bicarbonate of soda and cream of tartar into a bowl, stir in the wholemeal flour and sugar. Rub in the butter finely.

3 Stir in the buttermilk or fresh milk with baking powder and mix to a soft dough. Knead lightly on a floured surface.

4 Roll out or shape into a round about 17.5cm (7in) in diameter and place in the prepared container. Score to half the depth into 6 or 8 wedges. Dust with wholemeal flour.

5 Cook for $4\frac{1}{2}$–5 min. Serve hot or cold split into wedges, with butter.

Girdle scones *(makes 8–10)*

POWER LEVEL: 100% (FULL)

Traditionally cooked on a girdle, these microwave 'girdle' scones are cooked in a browning dish.

225g (8oz) plain flour
pinch salt
1 × 15ml tbsp (1 tbsp) baking powder
50g (2oz) butter or margarine
1 × 5ml tsp (1 tsp) sugar
150ml ($\frac{1}{4}$pt) milk or milk and water mixed
oil

1 Sift the flour, salt and baking powder into a bowl. Rub in the butter or margarine finely. Stir in the sugar and mix to a soft manageable dough with the milk.

2 Knead lightly on a floured surface and roll into a round approximately 6mm ($\frac{1}{4}$in) thick. Cut into rounds with a 5cm (2in) cutter or cut the large round into 8 triangles.

3 Preheat the browning dish for 4–5 min, depending on size. Lightly brush the base with oil.

4 Quickly place the scones in the browning dish, arranging the triangles with the pointed ends towards the centre.

5 Cook for 1 min, turn the scones over and the dish around, cook for $1\frac{1}{2}$–2 min.

6 Leave to cool on a wire rack. Serve hot or cold, split and buttered.

Sultana girdle scones (makes 8–10)

Follow the ingredients and method for girdle scones, adding 2 × 15ml heaped tbsp (2 heaped tbsp) sultanas to the dry ingredients.

Cheesy girdle scones (makes 8–10)

Follow the ingredients and method for girdle scones, omitting the sugar and adding 50g (2oz) grated cheddar cheese to the dry ingredients.

Summer Pudding (page 92)

Preserves

The advantages of cooking preserves in the microwave are that they can be made quickly with little fuss and bother, the flavours are enhanced, and particularly important with jams and marmalades, a very good colour is retained. In addition, the kitchen remains cooler and free of smells and it really is possible to make small quantities without the worry of the food sticking or burning onto the base of the cooking container.

Fresh fruit with a high pectin content – citrus fruits, gooseberries and blackcurrants – give best results. Fruit which is low in pectin – strawberries and apricots – should have citric acid, lemon juice or commercial pectin added.

Test your jams and marmalades for setting point in the normal way, by pouring a little onto a saucer and leaving it to cool for a few minutes. Setting point is reached if the skin formed on top of the preserve wrinkles when touched. Alternatively, a sugar thermometer can be used when the temperature should reach 105°C (220°F), although some fruits require a degree or two higher than this to obtain a satisfactory set. The thermometer should not be left in the oven when cooking unless specially designed for use in the microwave. Use a large heat-resistant dish or bowl for cooking – approximately 3l (6pt) – ensuring that there is enough room for expansion when the preserves are boiling.

The glass jars can be sterilized by adding a little water to each and heating in the microwave until the water is boiling rapidly. Drain the jars and pour in the preserve. Top with waxed discs and when completely cold, cover the jars with cellophane tops and label clearly.

Apricot jam *makes about $2\frac{1}{4}$kg (5lb)*
POWER LEVEL: 100% (FULL)

$1\frac{1}{2}$kg ($3\frac{1}{2}$lb) apricots
225ml (8fl oz) water
6g ($\frac{1}{4}$oz) citric acid
$1\frac{3}{4}$kg (4lb) preserving sugar

1 Wash, halve and stone the apricots. Place in a large glass bowl with the water and citric acid.
2 Cover with a lid or clingfilm slit with the pointed end of a sharp knife. Cook for 15–20 min, stirring 2–3 times throughout.

3 Add the sugar and stir well. Cook uncovered for 45–50 min, or until setting point is reached, stirring every 5–10 min.
4 Allow to stand for 20–30 min. Warm jars, then pot the jam, seal and label.

Blackcurrant jam *makes about 1kg (2lb)*
POWER LEVEL: 100% (FULL)

450g (1lb) blackcurrants
425ml ($\frac{3}{4}$pt) boiling water
675g ($1\frac{1}{2}$lb) preserving sugar

1 Remove stalks, wash the fruit, drain well and place in a large bowl with the boiling water.
2 Bring to the boil in the microwave then cook for about 5 min until the fruit is tender.
3 Stir in the sugar until dissolved.
4 Cook uncovered for 25–30 min or until setting point is reached, stirring every 5 min.
5 Allow to stand for 20 min and then pour into warmed jars. Seal and label.

Apple and ginger preserve *makes about 675g ($1\frac{1}{4}$lb)*
POWER LEVEL: 100% (FULL)

450g (1lb) cooking apples, washed
1 × 15ml tbsp (1 tbsp) lemon juice
6g ($\frac{1}{4}$oz) root ginger
275ml ($\frac{1}{2}$pt) water
450g (1lb) preserving sugar
100g (4oz) preserved ginger, finely chopped

1 Slice the apples without peeling and place in a large glass bowl with the lemon juice.
2 Bruise the ginger by hitting it with a rolling pin, then add it to the apples.
3 Add the water, cover with clingfilm and cook for 10 min. Remove the ginger.
4 Press the apples through a jelly cloth to extract all the juice. This should produce 550ml (1pt) of extract.
5 Add the sugar and preserved ginger to the extract. Stir until the sugar is dissolved. Cook uncovered for 25 min or until setting point is reached, stirring every 5 min.
6 Cool for 20–30 min, stir then pot, seal and label.

Lemon curd *makes about 1kg (2lb)*
POWER LEVEL: 100% (FULL)

175g (6oz) butter
4 eggs
2 egg yolks
275g (10oz) caster sugar
4 large lemons, grated rind and juice

1 Cut the butter into pieces and place in a large bowl. Heat for 4–5 min until melted.
2 Beat together the rest of the ingredients and stir into the butter.
3 Cook uncovered for 6–7 min, stirring every minute until thick enough to coat the back of a wooden spoon.
4 Pour the curd into small jars then seal and label.

Note: *Lemon curd does not keep well so is best made in small quantities and stored in a cool place for about 1 month.*

Strawberry jam *makes about 1½kg (3lb)*
POWER LEVEL: 100% (FULL)
colour page 107

1¾kg (3½lb) strawberries, hulled and washed
15g (½oz) citric acid
1¼kg (2¾lb) preserving sugar

1 Place the strawberries in a large bowl. Sprinkle with the citric acid and cook for about 15 min until soft.
2 Add the sugar and stir well. Cook the jam, uncovered, for 40 min or until setting point is reached. Stir the jam every 10 min at the beginning of cooking and every 5 min towards the end of the time.
3 Allow the jam to stand for 20–30 min. Pour into warmed jars, seal and label.

Hot 'n' spicy chutney *makes about 900g (2lb)*
POWER LEVEL: 100% (FULL)
colour page 107

450g (1lb) cooking apples, peeled, cored and sliced
1 large onion, chopped
1 clove garlic, finely chopped
25g (1oz) salt
225g (8oz) brown sugar
325ml (13fl oz) malt vinegar
225g (8oz) raisins
25g (1oz) ground ginger and dried mustard, mixed
½ × 5ml tsp (½ tsp) cayenne pepper

1 Place the apples, onion, garlic, salt and sugar in a large bowl with the malt vinegar.
2 Cover and cook for approximately 10 min or until soft.
3 Purée the mixture in a blender or pass through a sieve. Add the raisins.
4 Mix the spices with a little of the purée and add to the chutney. Leave to stand overnight, then pot, seal and label.

Note: *If preferred, all the ingredients may be cooked together and potted without puréeing.*

Three fruit marmalade *makes about 2½kg (5½lb)*

POWER LEVEL: 100% (FULL)
colour photograph opposite

2 grapefruit
2 large lemons
2 oranges
850ml (1½pt) boiling water
1.8kg (4lb) preserving sugar

1 Wash, dry and halve the fruit. Squeeze out the juice and place it in a large glass bowl.
2 Remove the pith and pips from the fruit skins and tie them in a piece of muslin or fine cloth. Shred the peel according to your preference – fine, medium or coarse.
3 Place the peel in the bowl with the juice and the bag of pith and pips. Add 275ml (½pt) boiling water and leave to stand for 1 hr. Remove the bag.
4 Add the rest of the boiling water. Cover with clingfilm and cook for 20–30 min, depending on the thickness of the peel.
5 Add the sugar and stir until dissolved. Cook, uncovered, for 25–30 min, stirring every 5 min until setting point is reached.
6 Allow the marmalade to stand for 30 min, then pot, seal and label.

Sweetcorn relish *makes about 1½kg (3lb)*

POWER LEVEL: 100% (FULL)
colour photograph opposite

1 × 5ml tsp (1 tsp) turmeric, or a few strands of saffron
225ml (8fl oz) distilled malt vinegar
1 red pepper, deseeded and diced
1 green pepper, deseeded and diced
1 stick celery, finely chopped
1 onion, peeled and finely chopped
1 clove garlic, finely chopped
675g (1½lb) sweetcorn kernels, fresh, frozen or canned
225g (8oz) caster sugar
pinch each mustard, mace, tarragon
2 × 15ml tbsp (2 tbsp) arrowroot, blended with a little water

1 Add the turmeric or saffron to the vinegar and leave to turn yellow while preparing the vegetables.
2 Strain the vinegar into a large bowl and add all the vegetables except the sweetcorn. Cover and cook for 5 min.
3 Add the sweetcorn, sugar and seasonings. Stir well and cook for 5 min.
4 Add the arrowroot blended with water to the mixture. Stir well and cook for 5 min, stir, then cook for 3 min or until thickened.
5 Leave to cool slightly then pot, seal and label.

Sweet damson pickle *makes about 1kg (2lb)*

POWER LEVEL: 50% (DEFROST) AND 100% (FULL)

900g (2lb) damsons, washed
rind ½ lemon
6 cloves
6 allspice seeds
small piece each root ginger and cinnamon stick
450g (1lb) brown sugar
275ml (½pt) vinegar

1 Place the whole damsons in a large bowl. Tie the lemon rind and spices in a muslin bag.
2 Dissolve the sugar in the vinegar and pour over the damsons.
3 Cover with a lid or clingfilm slit with the pointed end of a knife and cook on 50% (defrost) setting for 12–15 min until the damsons are tender.
4 Drain and reserve the vinegar; pack the fruit neatly into warmed jars.
5 Boil the vinegar in the microwave on 100% (full) setting until it is reduced to a thin syrup.
6 Pour over the fruit in the jars and seal and label immediately.

Selection of preserves

Date chutney *makes about 1¼kg (2½lb)*
POWER LEVEL: 100% (FULL)

450g (1lb) dates, roughly chopped
450g (1lb) raisins
1 medium onion, peeled and finely chopped
350g (12oz) brown sugar
2 cloves garlic, crushed
2 × 5ml tsp (2 tsp) salt
4–6 chillies, finely chopped
550ml (1pt) vinegar

1 Place all the ingredients in a large bowl and cover with a lid or clingfilm, slit with the pointed end of a sharp knife.
2 Bring the mixture to the boil and cook until tender and the desired consistency is reached, about 30 min.
3 Leave to cool slightly then pot, seal and label.

Rhubarb chutney *makes about 1½–2kg (3–4lb)*
POWER LEVEL: 100% (FULL)

1¼kg (2½lb) rhubarb, washed and cut into small pieces
225g (8oz) onions, peeled and finely chopped or minced
450g (1lb) sugar
6g (¼oz) ground ginger
25g (1oz) ground mixed spice
6g (¼oz) salt
425ml (¾pt) vinegar

1 Place the rhubarb, onions, sugar, spices and salt in a large bowl. Stir in 150ml (¼pt) of the vinegar.
2 Cover and cook for about 15 min, stirring every 5 min, until the rhubarb is tender.
3 Stir in the rest of the vinegar and cook uncovered until thick.
4 Pot, seal and label.

Breads

The advantage of proving dough in the microwave is that it is so fast – 450g (1lb) of white or brown bread dough can be proved in half the normal time required. The covered dough is given combinations of short bursts of microwave energy for 15 sec with standing or resting periods of 5–10 min, which allows an even distribution of warmth through the dough, ensuring a steady rise. After proving and shaping, the dough can be cooked by microwave in 6–7 min. This will produce a good-textured loaf with a soft crust. Of course it will not be browned as when baking conventionally, but if a crisper crust is preferred the dough can be partly cooked for 3–4 min in the microwave and then finished in a conventional oven preheated to a high temperature, for 8–10 min. Alternatively, the dough can be prepared and proved by microwave and afterwards completely cooked conventionally.

Loaves of bread and rolls which are to be proved and cooked in the microwave cooker must, of course, be placed in suitable microwave containers. The dough may be sprinkled with nibbed wheat, poppy seeds or sesame seeds for a more decorative finish.

Included in this section are some sweet yeast mixtures and a few breads which are leavened with soda rather than yeast.

Defrosting

Remember that textures of food affect thawing times and so a light vienna or french bread will thaw more quickly than the heavier-textured varieties. One roll or a slice of bread may be thawed in 10–25 sec, two would take 15–30 sec, and three 20–35 sec. Crumpets and slices of bread to be toasted may be cooked from the frozen state, whereas muffins and teacakes need to be thawed in the microwave for 10–20 sec before being cut and toasted or, if not toasted, leave them to stand for 2 min before serving. Loaves of bread should be given short cooking periods of 1–2 min followed by rest periods, repeated until the bread is thawed.

Sliced bread or rolls may be placed in cotton, linen or paper serviettes inside a wicker or straw basket, heated in the microwave and served direct to the luncheon or dining table.

White bread (makes 1 loaf)
POWER LEVEL: 100% (FULL)
colour page 111

This is a basic white bread dough which can also be used for pizzas or white rolls.

1 × 5ml tsp (1 tsp) sugar
275ml (½pt) water
1 × 5ml tsp (1 tsp) dried yeast
450g (1lb) plain flour
1 × 5ml tsp (1 tsp) salt
40g (1½oz) butter or margarine
poppy seeds or sesame seeds for sprinkling

1 Lightly grease a 15cm (6in) soufflé dish or 900g (2lb) loaf dish and line the base with greasproof paper.
2 Add the sugar to half the water and warm for 30 sec. Stir in the yeast and leave for 8–12 min to activate.
3 Sift the flour and salt into a bowl and warm for 30 sec. Rub in the butter or margarine finely.
4 Warm the rest of the water for 30 sec and add with the yeast to the flour, adding a little extra water if necessary to make a fairly soft dough. Knead thoroughly until the dough is smooth.
5 Place the dough in a bowl covered with clingfilm and prove by heating for 15 sec and leaving to stand for 5–10 min. Repeat this 3–4 times until the dough had doubled in size.
6 Turn the dough onto a lightly floured surface and knead well until smooth. Shape the dough and place in the prepared container and prove as described previously until double in size.
7 Lightly oil the top of the dough and sprinkle with poppy seeds or sesame seeds.
8 Cook for 5 min, turning once if necessary. Leave to stand for 10 min, then turn out and cool on a wire rack.

Alternative conventional bake
Place the dough in a greased loaf dish or tin. If a metal loaf tin is used, the second proving must be carried out conventionally in a warm place. Cook in a preheated oven at 220°C (425°F) Mark 7 for 20–30 min.

White rolls *(makes 16)*

POWER LEVEL: 100% (FULL)
colour page 111

These are made from the basic white bread dough.

450g (1lb) white bread dough (page 108)
poppy seeds or sesame seeds for sprinkling

1 Follow the instructions for white bread until the end of the first proving at stage 5.
2 Turn the dough onto a lightly floured surface and knead well until smooth.
3 Divide the dough into 16 pieces, shape the rolls and place in a circle on a lightly greased microwave baking tray or oven shelf.
4 Heat for 15 sec and leave to stand for 5–10 min. Repeat until the rolls have well risen.
5 Lightly brush the rolls with oil and sprinkle with poppy seeds or sesame seeds.
6 Cook 8 at a time for 2 min, rearranging the rolls if necessary halfway through. Leave to cool on a wire rack.

Alternative conventional bake
After the second proving on the microwave shelf, place the rolls on a lightly greased baking tray. Alternatively, prove on a baking tray in a warm place. Cook in a preheated oven at 220°C (425°F) Mark 7 for 15–20 min. For a more glossy finish, the rolls may be brushed with beaten egg before baking.

Alternative shapes for rolls
Plait: Divide dough into three, shape each piece into a long roll and plait together securing ends firmly.
Twist: Divide dough into two, shape each piece into a long roll and twist together, securing ends firmly.
Knot: Shape dough into a long roll and tie into a knot.
Rings: Shape dough into a long roll and bend it round to form a ring, dampen the ends and secure by moulding them together.

Prove and bake as described in the recipe.

Light wholemeal bread (makes 1 loaf) and rolls (makes 16)
colour page 111

Follow the ingredients and method for white bread and rolls, substituting 225g (8oz) of wholemeal flour for white flour and using sesame seeds or nibbed wheat instead of poppy seeds for sprinkling.

Note: *Wholemeal flours tend to absorb slightly less liquid than the finer flours which fact should be taken into account when mixing the dough, and the proving times may be slightly longer.*

Light rye bread *(makes 1 loaf)*

POWER LEVEL: 100% (FULL)

This closer-textured bread has good keeping qualities and is delicious with smoked fish and cheese.

$1\frac{1}{2}$ × 5ml tsp ($1\frac{1}{2}$ tsp) brown sugar
425ml ($\frac{3}{4}$pt) water, approximately
1 × 5ml tsp (1 tsp) dried yeast
450g (1lb) strong plain flour
100g (4oz) rye flour
$1\frac{1}{2}$ × 5ml tsp ($1\frac{1}{2}$ tsp) salt
caraway seeds or cumin seeds for sprinkling, optional

1 Lightly grease a 22cm (9in) round dish or a 900g (2lb) loaf dish and line the base with greaseproof paper.
2 Add the sugar to a third of the water and warm for 30 sec. Stir in the yeast and leave for 8–12 min to activate.
3 Mix the flours and salt well and warm for 30 sec. Warm the remaining liquid for 45 sec.
4 Add the yeast and sufficient of the remaining water to the flours to form a soft dough. Mix well, knead lightly and form into a ball.
5 Place the dough into a bowl covered with clingfilm and prove by heating for 15 sec and leaving to stand for 5–10 min. Repeat this process 3–4 times until the dough has doubled in size. If you have the time, knead and prove again.
6 Turn the dough onto a floured surface, knead well until smooth. Shape the dough and place into the prepared container.
7 With a sharp knife, make a cut across the top and widen this by pressing into it with the blade of the knife. Brush the top with oil, sprinkle with rye flour and a few caraway seeds or cumin seeds.
8 Prove as described previously until double in size. Cook for $5\frac{1}{2}$–$6\frac{1}{2}$ min, turning once halfway through if necessary. Leave for 10 min before turning out onto a wire rack to cool.

Note: *$1\frac{1}{2}$ × 5ml tsp ($1\frac{1}{2}$ tsp) caraway or cumin seeds may be added to the flours before mixing for the characteristic flavour of rye bread.*

Alternative conventional bake
Place the dough in a greased round ovenware dish or loaf tin. If a metal tin is used, the second proving must be carried out conventionally in a warm place. Cook in a preheated oven at 230°C (450°F) Mark 8 for 15 min, reduce to 190°C (375°F) Mark 5 for 15 min, reduce to 160°C (325°F) Mark 3 for a further 10 min or until cooked through.

Dark rye bread
colour page 111

Follow the ingredients and method for light rye bread using all rye flour.

Baps (*makes 6*)
POWER LEVEL: 100% (FULL)
colour photograph opposite

These are light rolls suitable as hamburger buns and make good alternatives to bread slices when making sandwiches.

450g (1lb) white bread dough (page 108)

1 Follow the instructions for white bread until the end of the first proving at stage 5.
2 Turn the dough onto a lightly floured surface and knead well until smooth.
3 Divide the dough into 6, knead each piece and roll into an oval shape.
4 Place 3 baps on the floured microwave baking tray or shelf, dust with flour. Heat for 15 sec and leave to stand for 5–10 min. Repeat until well risen.
5 Cook for 2 min, rearranging the baps if necessary halfway through. Leave to cool on a wire rack.
6 Repeat stages 4 and 5 with the remaining 3 baps.

Alternative conventional bake
Prove the 6 baps in the microwave then place on lightly floured baking trays. Alternatively, prove on a baking tray in a warm place. Cook in a preheated oven at 220°C (425°F) Mark 7 for 5 min, then reduce to 200°C (400°F) Mark 6 for a further 15–20 min. The baps should be pale brown when cooked.

Wholemeal bread (*makes 1 loaf*)
POWER LEVEL: 100% (FULL)

This is a coarser-textured wholemeal loaf.

$1\frac{1}{2}$ × 5ml tsp ($1\frac{1}{2}$ tsp) soft brown sugar
275ml ($\frac{1}{2}$pt) milk and water mixed, approximately
1 × 5ml tsp (1 tsp) dried yeast
450g (1lb) wholemeal flour
2 × 5ml tsp (2 tsp) salt
40g ($1\frac{1}{2}$oz) butter or margarine
nibbed wheat for sprinkling

1 Lightly grease a 20cm (8in) flan dish and line the base with greaseproof paper.
2 Add the sugar to half the water and warm for 30 sec. Stir in the yeast and leave for 8–12 min to activate.
3 Place the flour and salt in a bowl and warm for 30 sec. Rub in the butter or margarine finely. Warm the rest of the liquid for 30 sec.
4 Add the yeast and warmed liquid to the flour. Mix well. This should be a soft dough and the quantity of liquid required may vary slightly. Knead thoroughly until the dough is smooth.
5 Place the dough in a bowl covered with clingfilm and prove by heating for 15 sec and leaving to stand for 5–10 min. Repeat this process 3–4 times until the dough has doubled in size.

6 Turn the dough onto a lightly floured surface and knead well until smooth. Shape the dough and place in the prepared container and prove as described previously until double in size.
7 Lightly oil the top of the dough and sprinkle with nibbed wheat.
8 Cook for 5 min, turning once halfway through if necessary. Leave to stand for 10 min and then turn out onto a wire rack to cool.

Alternative conventional bake
Place the dough in a greased flan dish or sandwich tin. If a metal tin is used, the second proving must be carried out conventionally in a warm place. Cook in a preheated oven at 200°C (400°F) Mark 6 for 35–45 min.

Onion bread (*makes 1 loaf*)
POWER LEVEL: 100% (FULL)

Delicious when eaten with salad or hot soup.

1 × 5ml tsp (1 tsp) sugar
375ml (12fl oz) water
2 × 5ml tsp (2 tsp) dried yeast
450g (1lb) plain flour
1 × 5ml tsp (1 tsp) salt
40g ($1\frac{1}{2}$oz) butter or margarine
3 × 15ml tbsp (3 tbsp) dried onion soup mix

1 Lightly grease a 15cm (6in) soufflé dish and line the base with greaseproof paper.
2 Add the sugar to half the water and warm for 30 sec. Stir in the yeast and leave to activate for 8–12 min.
3 Sift the flour and salt and warm for 30 sec. Rub in the butter finely, stir in the onion soup mix, reserving 2 × 5ml tsp (2 tsp). Warm the rest of the water for 30 sec.
4 Add the yeast and warm water to the flour. Mix well and knead until smooth.
5 Place the dough in a bowl and cover with clingfilm. Prove by heating for 15 sec and leaving to rest for 5–10 min. Repeat 3–4 times until the dough has doubled in size.
6 Knead on a floured surface, shape the dough and place in the prepared container. Prove as described previously and when doubled in size lightly oil the top and sprinkle with the remaining soup mix.
7 Cook for 5 min, turning once halfway through if necessary. Leave for 10–15 min before removing onto a wire rack to cool.

Alternative conventional bake
Place the dough in a greased, ovenproof dish or 450g (1lb) loaf tin. If a metal tin is used, the second proving must be carried out conventionally in a warm place. Cook in a preheated oven at 200°C (400°F) Mark 6 for about 45 min.

Garlic bread

POWER LEVEL: 100% (FULL)

1 short, crusty french stick
150g (5oz) butter, softened
3–4 cloves garlic, crushed or finely chopped, or
1–1½ × 5ml tsp (1–1½ tsp) garlic powder

1 Cut the loaf, not quite through, into slices 2.5cm (1in) thick.
2 Cream the butter and beat in the garlic.
3 Spread a large knob of butter between the slices.
4 Protect the thin ends of the loaf with small, smooth pieces of aluminium foil.
5 Place on kitchen paper in the microwave cooker and cover with a piece of damp kitchen paper.
6 Cook for 1½ min or until the butter has just melted and bread is warmed through.

Herb bread
Follow the ingredients and method for garlic bread substituting 1 × 15ml tbsp (1 tbsp) finely chopped fresh mixed herbs or 2 × 5ml tsp (2 tsp) dried mixed herbs for the garlic.

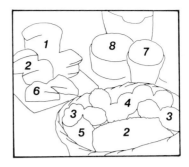

Selection of breads and rolls:
1 *Dark Rye Bread (page 109)*
2 *Light Wholemeal Bread (page 109)*
3 *White Rolls (page 109)*
4 *Light Wholemeal Rolls (page 109)*
5 *Baps (page 110)*
6 *Oatmeal Bread (page 112)*
7 *Cheese Bread (page 112)*
8 *White Bread (page 108)*

Oatmeal bread (*makes 1 loaf*)
POWER LEVEL: 100% (FULL)
colour page 111

275g (10oz) plain flour
175g (6oz) rolled oats
1 × 5ml tsp (1 tsp) salt
1 × 5ml tsp (1 tsp) bicarbonate of soda
1 × 5ml tsp (1 tsp) cream of tartar
100g (4oz) butter or margarine
1 × 15ml tbsp (1 tbsp) caster sugar
275ml (½pt) buttermilk or soured milk, approximately
rolled oats for sprinkling

1 Lightly grease a 22cm (9in) round dish and line the base with greaseproof paper; sprinkle with oats.
2 Sift the flour, mix in the oats, salt and raising agents. Rub in the butter finely, mix in the sugar.
3 Add sufficient of the milk to mix to a light scone dough. Knead lightly on a floured surface and shape into a round about 2.5cm (1in) thick.
4 Place into the prepared container. Score or cut into 8 wedges and sprinkle the top with oats.
5 Cook for 5 min, turning once halfway through. If necessary, test with a skewer and give an extra minute if not quite cooked.
6 Leave for 10–15 min before turning onto a wire rack to cool.

Alternative conventional bake
Cook in a round ovenware dish or tin in a preheated oven at 200°C (400°F) Mark 6 for 30–35 min.

Cheese bread (*makes 1 loaf*)
POWER LEVEL: 100% (FULL)
colour page 111

175g (6oz) cheddar cheese finely grated
1 × 5ml tsp (1 tsp) sugar
275ml (½pt) water
1 × 5ml tsp (1 tsp) dried yeast
450g (1lb) plain flour
1 × 5ml tsp (1 tsp) salt
½ × 5ml tsp (½ tsp) dried mustard
½ × 5ml tsp (½ tsp) pepper
1 × 5ml tsp (1 tsp) celery salt, optional

1 Dampen the inside of a 15cm (6in) soufflé dish and sprinkle with 1 × 15ml tbsp (1 tbsp) of the finely grated cheese. There is no need to grease the dish.
2 Add the sugar to half the water and warm for 30 sec. Stir in the yeast and leave to activate for 8–12 min.
3 Sift the flour and seasonings and warm for 30 sec. Warm the rest of the water for 30 sec.
4 Reserving 1 × 15ml tbsp (1 tbsp), stir the rest of the cheese into the flour. Add the yeast and warm water. Mix well and knead until smooth.
5 Place the dough in a bowl, cover with clingfilm and prove by heating for 15 sec and leaving to stand for 5–10 min. Repeat until it has doubled in size.
6 Knead on a floured surface, shape the dough and place in the prepared container. Prove as described previously until doubled in size. Sprinkle the top with the remaining cheese and celery salt, if using.
7 Cook for 5–6 min, turning once halfway through if necessary.
8 Leave for 10–15 min before turning out onto a wire rack to cool.

Alternative conventional bake
Place the dough in a greased, ovenproof dish or 450g (1lb) loaf tin. If a metal tin is used, the second proving must be carried out conventionally in a warm place. Cook in a preheated oven at 200°C (400°F) Mark 6 for approximately 45 min.

Soda bread (*makes 1 loaf*)
POWER LEVEL: 100% (FULL)

This bread is leavened with soda rather than yeast.

450g (1lb) plain flour
1 × 5ml tsp (1 tsp) salt
1 × 5ml tsp (1 tsp) bicarbonate of soda
1 × 5ml tsp (1 tsp) cream of tartar
50g (2oz) butter or margarine
350ml (12fl oz) buttermilk or soured milk

1 Lightly grease and flour a 22cm (9in) round dish and line the base with floured, greaseproof paper.
2 Sift the flour, salt and raising agents into a bowl. Rub in the butter finely.
3 Add the milk and mix to a soft dough. Knead lightly on a floured surface and shape or roll into a large round about 2.5cm (1in) thick.
4 Place the dough into the prepared dish and sprinkle the top with flour. Score or cut into 8 wedges.
5 Cook for 5 min, turn the dish, cook for 1–2 min. Leave for 10–15 min before turning out to cool on a wire rack.

Alternative conventional bake
Cook in a round ovenware dish or tin in a preheated oven at 200°C (400°F) Mark 6 for 25–30 min.

Brown soda bread

Follow the ingredients and method for soda bread substituting 225g (8oz) of wholemeal for white flour.

Fly bread

Follow the ingredients and method for soda bread adding 50g (2oz) currants and 25g (1oz) caster sugar to the dry ingredients.

Honey Baked Apples (page 92) and Apple and Damson Tansy (page 89)

Savarin (page 115)

Pizza napolitana
POWER LEVEL: 100% (FULL)

450g (1lb) pizza dough (see below)
550ml (1pt) tomato sauce (page 47)
350g (12oz) mozzarella cheese
50g (2oz) can anchovy fillets
75–100g (3–4oz) black olives
1–2 × 5ml tsp (1–2 tsp) dried herbs, eg oregano, basil or majoram
2 × 15ml tbsp (2 tbsp) olive oil, approximately

1 Follow the method for the pizza dough. When the dough has been shaped and proved for the second time, add the topping as follows.
2 Spread each round of dough liberally with the tomato sauce. Cover with the cheese which has been thinly sliced, the drained anchovy fillets which have been split in two lengthways, and the black olives.
3 Sprinkle with the herbs and the olive oil (about 1–2 × 5ml tsp/1–2 tsp for each pizza).
4 Cook the smaller pizzas for 5–6 min each, the larger ones for 7–8 min each, giving a quarter turn every 1½ min.

Variations
Pizza alla romana Omit the tomato sauce and anchovies and replace with extra mozzarella cheese and sprinkle liberally with grated parmesan cheese and fresh basil.
Pizza aglioe olio Omit the tomato sauce and cheese and replace with liberal amounts of crushed or finely chopped garlic, olive oil and chopped marjoram.
Onion pizza Follow the ingredients for pizza napolitana but add some lightly sautéed onion rings to the top with the anchovies and olives.
Mushroom pizza Omit the anchovies and olives and replace with lightly sautéed sliced mushrooms.

Seafood pizza Omit the cheese and replace with shelled mussels or prawns; sprinkle with oregano and chopped parsley (*colour page 117*).
American pizza Follow the ingredients for pizza napolitana, adding slices of salami on top of the cheese and slices of red pepper, lightly sautéed in oil.
Ham pizza Follow the ingredients for pizza napolitana adding some sliced ham and mortadella sausage which have been thinly shredded (*colour page 117*).

Pizza dough (*makes 3 large or 4 smaller pizzas*)
POWER LEVEL: 100% (FULL)

1 × 5ml tsp (1 tsp) sugar
275ml (½pt) water, approximately
2 × 5ml tsp (2 tsp) dried yeast
450g (1lb) plain flour
1½ × 5ml tsp (1½ tsp) salt
3 × 15ml tbsp (3 tbsp) olive oil

1 Lightly grease 3–4 × 20–25cm (8–10in) plates.
2 Add the sugar to half the water and heat for 30 sec. Stir in the yeast and leave for 8–12 min to activate.
3 Sift the flour and salt and warm for 30 sec, warm the rest of the water for 30 sec.
4 Add the yeast mixture to the flour and mix to a soft dough with the rest of the water, adjusting the quantity if necessary. When the mixture is smooth, turn onto a floured surface and knead well.
5 Place the dough in a bowl, cover with clingfilm and prove by heating for 15 sec, then letting it rest for 5–10 min. Repeat 3–4 times until dough is double in size.
6 Knead the dough again, this time working in the oil, a little at a time until all the oil is absorbed and the dough is pliable and smooth.
7 Shape the dough by rolling or pressing into 3 larger or 4 smaller rounds to fit the prepared plates. Prove each round separately in rotation in the microwave as described above until well risen.

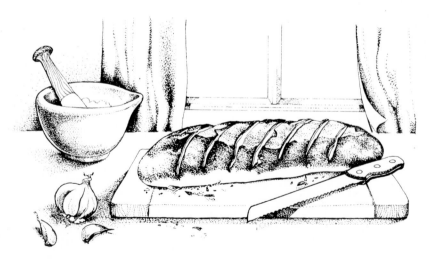

Savarin (*serves 8*)

POWER LEVEL: 100% (FULL)

colour page 113

1 × 5ml tsp (1 tsp) sugar
150ml ($\frac{1}{4}$pt) water, approximately
2 × 5ml tsp (2 tsp) dried yeast
225g (8oz) plain flour
$\frac{1}{2}$ × 5ml tsp ($\frac{1}{2}$ tsp) salt
50g (2oz) butter or margarine
2 eggs, beaten
25g (1oz) flaked almonds
For serving:
syrup
apricot glaze
whipped cream
fruit salad

1 Lightly grease a 20cm (8in) microwave ring mould.
2 Add the sugar to the water and warm for 30 sec. Stir in the yeast and leave for 8–12 min to activate.
3 Sift the flour and salt and warm for 15 sec. Add the yeast mixture and a little more water if necessary. Mix and knead well; the dough should be fairly soft.
4 Cover and prove by heating for 10 sec and leaving to stand for 5 min. Repeat until the dough has doubled in size.
5 Melt the butter for 1$\frac{1}{2}$ min. Beat the butter and eggs into the dough until it resembles a thick batter. Beat well.
6 Arrange the flaked almonds in the base of the container and carefully pour in the batter.
7 Cover with clingfilm and prove as described earlier until the mixture is well risen in the mould.
8 Remove the clingfilm and cook for 6$\frac{1}{2}$–7 min, turning once halfway through.
9 Leave to cool for a few minutes before turning onto a cooling rack.
10 While still warm, pour the syrup over the savarin and when cool, brush with apricot glaze.
11 To serve, fill the centre with mixed fruit salad and decorate with swirls of whipped cream.

DO NOT FREEZE WITH THE FRUIT SALAD. FILL AND DECORATE JUST BEFORE SERVING

Syrup

POWER LEVEL: 100% (FULL)

100g (4oz) caster sugar
150ml ($\frac{1}{4}$pt) water
1 × 5ml tsp (1 tsp) lemon juice
2 × 15ml tbsp (2 tbsp) kirsch

1 Add the sugar to the water and heat for 1 min. Stir until the sugar is dissolved. Bring to the boil in the microwave and cook until a thick syrup is formed.
2 Stir in the lemon juice and kirsch and pour over the savarin while warm.

Apricot glaze

POWER LEVEL: 100% (FULL)

450g (1lb) apricot jam
2 × 15ml tbsp (2 tbsp) lemon juice
4 × 15ml tbsp (4 tbsp) water

Place all the ingredients in a bowl. Mix well together and then bring to the boil in the microwave. Allow to boil for 2–3 min, stirring frequently. Sieve and allow to cool and thicken slightly before use. This keeps very well in a covered jar so can be made in large quantities.

Chelsea buns (*makes 8*)

POWER LEVEL: 100% (FULL)

450g (1lb) white bread dough (page 108)
25g (1oz) butter
150g (5oz) currants
50g (2oz) soft brown sugar
soft brown sugar for sprinkling
pinch cinnamon or mixed spice
apricot glaze for top (above)

1 Lightly grease a large shallow dish.
2 Follow the instructions and method for the basic white bread dough until the end of the first proving.
3 Knead the dough on a floured surface. Roll out to a rectangle approximately 30 × 22.5cm (12 × 9in).
4 Melt the butter for 1 min and brush over the dough. Sprinkle over the currants and 50g (2oz) sugar. Roll up from one of the long sides like a swiss roll.
5 Cut into 8 slices and place side by side around the edge and middle of the prepared container. Prove as before until double in size. Sprinkle with the sugar and cinnamon or mixed spice.
6 Cook for 6–8 min, turning once halfway through if necessary. Leave to stand for 5–10 min before removing to a cooling rack.
7 Brush with hot apricot glaze.

Alternative conventional bake
Place the slices into a large greased shallow dish or tin. If a metal tin is used, the second proving must be carried out conventionally in a warm place. Cook in a preheated oven at 220°C (425°F) Mark 7 for 20–25 min.

Malt loaf (*makes 1*)
POWER LEVEL: 100% (FULL)

1 × 5ml tsp (1 tsp) soft brown sugar
150ml (¼pt) milk
2 × 5ml tsp (2 tsp) dried yeast
100g (4oz) wholemeal flour
100g (4oz) strong white flour
1 × 5ml tsp (1 tsp) salt
40g (1½oz) butter or margarine
1 × 5ml tbsp (1 tbsp) dark soft brown sugar
50g (2oz) currants
50g (2oz) sultanas
25g (1oz) chopped peel
2 × 15ml tbsp (2 tbsp) malt
½ × 15ml tbsp (½ tbsp) black treacle
oil for brushing
apricot glaze (page 114)

1 Lightly grease and line the base of a 15cm (6in) soufflé dish or a 900g (2lb) microwave loaf dish.
2 Add 1 × 5ml tsp (1 tsp) sugar to half the milk and warm for 15–20 sec. Stir in the yeast and leave to activate for 8–12 min.
3 Sift the flours and salt into a bowl and warm for 15–20 sec. Rub in the butter or margarine finely and stir in the brown sugar. Add the currants, sultanas and chopped peel.
4 Add the malt and black treacle to the rest of the milk and warm for 30 sec. Add to the flours with the yeast and mix well together until the dough is smooth.
5 Place in the prepared container. Brush the top of the dough lightly with the oil and cover the dish with clingfilm.
6 Prove by heating for 15 sec and allowing to stand for 5–10 min. Repeat until the dough has doubled in size. (This rich mixture may take longer to rise.)
7 Remove the clingfilm and cook for 4–5 min.
8 Leave for 5–10 min before turning onto a cooling rack. While still warm, brush the top and sides with hot apricot glaze.
9 Slice when cold and serve with butter.

Note: *This loaf improves if kept wrapped for a day before serving.*

Alternative conventional bake
Place in a greased soufflé dish or loaf dish (not metal) and after proving in the microwave, cook in a preheated oven 230°C (450°F) Mark 8 for 10 min, reduce to 190°C (375°F) Mark 5 for 25–30 min. Alternatively, prove in a metal container in a warm place, then cook as above.

Acknowledgements

I should like to thank Cathy Morton-Lloyd, Kate Pike and Anne Ross for their assistance in testing the recipes and preparing the food for the photographs. To Thorn EMI Domestic Electrical Appliances Ltd I offer my grateful thanks for supplying Tricity and Moffat microwave cookers and assisting with the photography and line drawings. Colour photography by John Plimmer, RPM Photographic, Havant. Line illustrations by KPA Advertising Ltd, Kettering, Northants.

Seafood Pizza (page 114) and Ham Pizza (page 114)

Index